# VIRGINIA
# WOOLF

COMPREHENSIVE RESEARCH
AND STUDY GUIDE

# BLOOM'S

## MAJOR

# NOVELISTS

**EDITED AND WITH AN
INTRODUCTION BY HAROLD BLOOM**

## BLOOM'S MAJOR DRAMATISTS

Aeschylus

Anton Chekhov

Aristophanes

Berthold Brecht

Euripides

Henrik Ibsen

Ben Jonson

Christopher
  Marlowe

Arthur Miller

Eugene O'Neill

Shakespeare's
  Comedies

Shakespeare's
  Histories

Shakespeare's
  Romances

Shakespeare's
  Tragedies

George Bernard
  Shaw

Neil Simon

Sophocles

Tennessee
  Williams

August Wilson

## BLOOM'S MAJOR NOVELISTS

Jane Austen

The Brontës

Willa Cather

Stephen Crane

Charles Dickens

Fyodor Dostoevsky

William Faulkner

F. Scott Fitzgerald

Thomas Hardy

Nathaniel Hawthorne

Ernest Hemingway

Henry James

James Joyce

D. H. Lawrence

Toni Morrison

John Steinbeck

Stendhal

Leo Tolstoy

Mark Twain

Alice Walker

Edith Wharton

Virginia Woolf

## BLOOM'S MAJOR WORLD POETS

Geoffrey Chaucer

Emily Dickinson

John Donne

T. S. Eliot

Robert Frost

Langston Hughes

John Milton

Edgar Allan Poe

Shakespeare's Poems
  & Sonnets

Alfred, Lord
  Tennyson

Walt Whitman

William Wordsworth

## BLOOM'S MAJOR SHORT STORY WRITERS

William Faulkner

F. Scott Fitzgerald

Ernest Hemingway

O. Henry

James Joyce

Herman Melville

Flannery O'Connor

Edgar Allan Poe

J. D. Salinger

John Steinbeck

Mark Twain

Eudora Welty

# VIRGINIA
# WOOLF

COMPREHENSIVE RESEARCH
AND STUDY GUIDE

## BLOOM'S
### MAJOR
## NOVELISTS

EDITED AND WITH AN INTRODUCTION
BY HAROLD BLOOM

First Printing
1 3 5 7 9 8 6 4 2

Library of Congress Cataloging-in-Publication Data
applied for

ISBN 0-7910-6344-5




Chelsea House Publishers
1974 Sproul Road, Suite 400
Broomall, PA 19008-0914

The Chelsea House World Wide Web address is
http://www.chelseahouse.com

Series Editor: Matt Uhler

Contributing Editor: Aaron Tillman

Produced by Publisher's Services, Santa Barbara, California

# Contents

# User's Guide

This volume is designed to present biographical, critical, and bibliographical information on the author's best-known or most important works. Following Harold Bloom's editor's note and introduction is a detailed biography of the author, discussing major life events and important literary accomplishments. A plot summary of each novel follows, tracing significant themes, patterns, and motifs in the work.

A selection of critical extracts, derived from previously published material from leading critics, analyzes aspects of each work. The extracts consist of statements from the author, if available, early reviews of the work, and later evaluations up to the present. A bibliography of the author's writings (including a complete list of all works written, cowritten, edited, and translated), a list of additional books and articles on the author and his or her work, and an index of themes and ideas in the author's writings conclude the volume.

~

**Harold Bloom** is Sterling Professor of the Humanities at Yale University and Henry W. and Albert A. Berg Professor of English at the New York University Graduate School. He is the author of over 20 books, including *Shelley's Mythmaking* (1959), *The Visionary Company* (1961), *Blake's Apocalypse* (1963), *Yeats* (1970), *A Map of Misreading* (1975), *Kabbalah and Criticism* (1975), *Agon: Toward a Theory of Revisionism* (1982), *The American Religion* (1992), *The Western Canon* (1994), and *Omens of Millennium: The Gnosis of Angels, Dreams, and Resurrection* (1996). *The Anxiety of Influence* (1973) sets forth Professor Bloom's provocative theory of the literary relationships between the great writers and their predecessors. His most recent books include *Shakespeare: The Invention of the Human,* a 1998 National Book Award finalist, and *How to Read and Why,* which was published in 2000.

Professor Bloom earned his Ph.D. from Yale University in 1955 and has served on the Yale faculty since then. He is a 1985 MacArthur Foundation Award recipient, served as the Charles Eliot Norton Professor of Poetry at Harvard University in 1987–88, and has received honorary degrees from the universities of Rome and Bologna. In 1999, Professor Bloom received the prestigious American Academy of Arts and Letters Gold Medal for Criticism.

Currently, Harold Bloom is the editor of numerous Chelsea House volumes of literary criticism, including the series BLOOM'S NOTES, BLOOM'S MAJOR DRAMATISTS, BLOOM'S MAJOR NOVELISTS, MAJOR LITERARY CHARACTERS, MODERN CRITICAL VIEWS, MODERN CRITICAL INTERPRETATIONS, and WOMEN WRITERS OF ENGLISH AND THEIR WORKS.

# Editor's Note

My Introduction is an overview of Woolf's achievement, centering upon her deep affinities with Walter Pater.

There are two dozen critical views of four Woolfian novels gathered together in this little volume.

On *Mrs. Dalloway,* Allen McLaurin shows how much more general Woolf's allusions are than Joyce's, while Manly Johnson exposes the mania of mind-control in the novel's "healers," and Mitchell A. Leaska ponders the enigma of just *how* Septimus can be Clarissa's double?

Howard Harper notes the single reference to Clarissa's mother, after which Judy Little finds in Clarissa's party a creative self-expression, and Emily Jensen centers upon the heroine's love for Sally Seton.

On *To the Lighthouse,* Thomas A. Vogler emphasizes the life-affirming drive both in Mrs. Ramsay and Lily, while Mitchell A. Leaska examines shared internal monologues, and Susan Rubinow Gorsky sketches the novel as a play in two acts.

Louise A. DeSalvo relates the novel to an episode when Woolf was fifteen, after which Susan Dick explores memory in *To the Lighthouse,* and Alice van Buren Kelley finds in Roger Fry's account of "significant form" a link to Woolf's concept of art.

*Orlando* is seen by Jean Guiguet as evidence of Woolf's withdrawal from "mere femininity," while Avrom Fleishman studies the novel's systematic incorporation of literary texts, and T. E. Apter finds limitations in Woolf's feminist criticism of male society.

For Judy Little, the feminist issue is handled superbly by Woolf, after which Patricia Clements sees the Great Frost scene as an image of desire and betrayal, and Madeleine Moore relates *Orlando* to Woolf's essay, "The Narrow Bridge of Art."

*Between the Acts* is judged by Joan Bennett to fuse aspects of poetry and the novel, while Alice van Buren Kelley finds in the book an affirmation of the unity of all other people and times, and Allen McLaurin finds both Roger Fry and Coleridge to be influences upon the book.

Susan Rubinow Gorsky emphasizes the bleakness of *Between the Acts,* after which Sallie Sears also notes the lack of living contact between persons, and Evelyn Haller demonstrates the book's use of Egyptian mythology.

# Introduction

## HAROLD BLOOM

Virginia Woolf was one of the most original novelists of the century now passed. Her life was a long, heroic struggle against madness. Her first breakdown was precipitated, at thirteen, by the death of her mother. The death of her father, Leslie Stephen, when she was twenty-two, stimulated a second breakdown and an attempted suicide. A third crisis lasted for three years, from thirty to thirty-three. Finally, under the terrible stress of German air bombardment, Woolf drowned herself at the age of fifty-nine.

Woolf's major novels, by common consent, are *Mrs. Dalloway* (1925) and *To the Lighthouse* (1927). *Orlando* (1928) remains popular, but is a secondary work. Her later novels are all extraordinary work, and clearly will survive: *The Waves* (1931), *The Years* (1937), and a final masterpiece, *Between the Acts* (1941). Formally speaking, Woolf's finest novel is *To the Lighthouse,* which is a miraculous concentration of her varied gifts.

Woolf has become the high priestess of feminist literary criticism, since she insists that the creative power of women "differs greatly from the creative power of man." Iris Murdoch refreshingly disagreed: "I think there's human experience; and I don't think a woman's mind differs essentially from a man's." There are major male novelists—Samuel Richardson, Tolstoy, Henry James—who have explored female consciousness perhaps more fully than did Jane Austen and Virginia Woolf. One can add Marcel Proust and James Joyce, whose depictions of inwardness are equally strong, whether women or men are being portrayed.

Woolf sought her precursors in Jane Austen and Emily Brontë, but in temperament and artistic stance she scarcely resembles either. The true precursor, as Perry Meisel has shown, was Walter Pater, whose sensibility hovers everywhere in Woolf. Her profound aestheticism is precisely Paterian: perception and sensation are what matter most as we face the universe of death. Woolf's relation to Pater is analogous to Proust's with Ruskin. Pater's *Imaginary Portraits* already are Woolfian, as Ruskin's *Praeterita* is Proustian.

Feminist critics have not confronted the difficulties of reconciling Woolf's aestheticism with their ideological means-test for literature. Except for her aestheticism, the author of *Mrs. Dalloway* and *To the Lighthouse* would be wholly nihilistic, which is true also of Pater, Ruskin, and Proust. Woolf teaches perception, and not politics. Her "androgyny" is not a pragmatic cause, but a fusion of perception and sensation with her acceptance of death and meaninglessness, apart from the flow of momentary meanings that art can suggest.

Woolf's ambivalence towards James Joyce betrays the anxiety of a common ancestry in Paterian solipsism, with its reliance upon epiphanies or privileged moments. Woolf's father, the empiricist Leslie Stephen, loathed Pater, and as Mr. Ramsay in *To the Lighthouse*, utters a rugged motto: "The very stone one kicks with one's boot will outlast Shakespeare."

Clarissa Dalloway, staring at herself in the mirror, saves herself from the madness that destroys Septimus, her daemon or soul's brother, by a Paterian vision of the self, crystal and diamond. As readers, we accept the reality of Mrs. Dalloway's self because of her marvelously articulated memories, which Woolf had the cunning to invent so as to give her character some distancing from Woolf herself:

> No, Lytton does not like Mrs. Dalloway, &, what is odd, I like him all the better for saying so, & don't much mind. What he says is that there is a discordancy between the ornament (extremely beautiful) & what happens (rather ordinary—or unimportant). This is caused he thinks by some discrepancy in Clarissa herself; he thinks remarkably, with myself. So that I think as a whole, the book does not ring solid; yet, he says, it is a whole; & he says sometimes the writing is of extreme beauty. What can one call it but genius? he said! Coming when, one never can tell. Fuller of genius, he said than anything I had done. Perhaps, he said, you have not yet mastered your method. You should take something wilder & more fantastic, a frame work that admits of anything, like Tristram Shandy. But then I should lose touch with emotions, I said. Yes, he agreed, there must be reality for you to start from. Heaven knows how you're to do it. But he thought me at the beginning, not at the end. And he said the C.R. {The Common Reader} was divine, a classic; Mrs. D. being, I fear, a flawed

stone. This is very personal, he said & old fashioned perhaps; yet I think there is some truth in it. For I remember the night at Rodmell when I decided to give it up, because I found Clarissa in some way tinselly. Then I invented her memories. But I think some distaste for her persisted. Yet, again, that was true to my feelings for Kitty {Maxse}, & one must dislike people in art without its mattering, unless indeed it is true that certain characters detract from the importance of what happens to them.

"A flawed stone" or a diamond: which is the accurate judgment upon Clarissa Dalloway? If she is a diamond, then it is only because of the extraordinary doubling between her and Septimus Smith, who will never meet one another. They share a single consciousness, precariously on the edge of life. Septimus dies Clarissa's death for her:

> She had once thrown a shilling into the Serpentine, never anything more. But he had flung it away. They went on living (she would have to go back; the rooms were still crowded; people kept on coming). They (all day she had been thinking of Bourton, of Peter, of Sally), they would grow old. A thing there was that mattered; a thing, wreathed about with chatter, defaced, obscured in her own life, let drop every day in corruption, lies, chatter. This he had preserved. Death was defiance. Death was an attempt to communicate; people feeling the impossibility of reaching the centre which, mystically, evaded them; closeness drew apart; rapture faded, one was alone. There was an embrace in death.

Suicide is a communication, since the mystical center otherwise evades us. Direct experience, in life or in literature, recedes from us, the more eagerly we seek for it. Woolf's novels forsake the naturalism that alienated her in James Joyce, in favor—not of symbolism—but of Pater's impressionism. ❀

# Biography of
# Virginia Woolf

Adeline Virginia Stephen was born in London on January 25, 1882. She was the third child, after Vanessa and Thoby, of Leslie Stephen and Julia Duckworth Stephen. The following year, the last of Virginia's siblings, Adrian Leslie Stephen, was born.

In 1895, Virginia's mother died. Soon after her death, Virginia experienced her first significant breakdown. Two years later, after she began to study Greek at King's College, her stepsister, Stella Duckworth, died. In 1904, her father was knighted. Two years later he died, and Virginia experienced her second significant breakdown. Later that year she moved to 46 Gordon Square, Bloomsbury, and published her first piece, a review in *The Guardian*.

In 1906, her brother Thoby Stephen died of typhoid. The following year, Virginia and Adrian moved to 29 Fitzroy Square where she began her first novel. In 1911, Virginia and her brother shared a house with John Maynard Keynes, Duncan Grant, and Leonard Woolf. On August 10 of the following year, she married Leonard Woolf.

In 1913, Virginia completed her first novel, *The Voyage Out*, but publication had to be delayed because of another breakdown and a suicide attempt. Her novel was finally published in 1915. By 1917, Virginia was contributing regularly to the *Times Literary Supplement*, while working on her second novel, *Night and Day*. In 1918, she met T. S. Eliot for the first time. Later that year she published *Kew Gardens*. The following year she printed some of Eliot's poems in her printing press in Hogarth House.

In 1920, Virginia began working on *Jacob's Room*. The following year, *Monday or Tuesday* was published. In 1922, stricken by ill health, she met Mrs. Harold Nicholson (Vita Sackville-West), who was the inspiration for her novel *Orlando. Jacob's Room* was published that same year. In 1923, her friend and artistic peer Katherine Mansfield died. That same year her husband Leonard became literary editor of *The Nation* and Virginia began work on *Mrs. Dalloway*. Virginia and her husband moved to Bloomsbury in 1924. It was where she completed her work on *Mrs. Dalloway*, which was published the following year.

In 1926, Virginia began working on *To the Lighthouse*. This novel was published in 1927. During this year, she started visiting Vita Sackville-West on a regular basis and began her work on the novel *Orlando*. In 1928, *Orlando* was published and she was awarded the Femina Vie Heureuse prize. The following year, *A Room of One's Own,* her Cambridge lectures, were published. During this year she started work on *The Waves,* which was published in 1931.

In 1932, *A Letter to a Young Poet* and *The Common Reader: Second Series* were published. In 1933, Virginia refused an honorary doctorate and declined the Leslie Stephen lectureship at Cambridge. That same year, *Flush: A Biography* was published and she began working on *The Years.*

In 1936, she began work on *Three Guineas* and compiled material for her biography of Roger Fry. The following year, *The Years* was published and Julian Bell was killed in the Spanish Civil War. *Three Guineas* was published in 1938. The following year she met Sigmund Freud for the first time.

In 1940, she read a paper in Brighton to the Workers' Educational Association that was later published as 'The Leaning Tower.' That same year, *Roger Fry: A Biography* was published. In 1941, after completing her final novel *Between the Acts*, Virginia drowned herself in a river near Monk's House where she had lived in 1919. ❀

# Plot Summary of
## *Mrs. Dalloway*

*Mrs. Dalloway,* a novel in which the narrative present spans only one day, opens on a summer morning as Clarissa Dalloway leaves her Westminster home to buy flowers for a party that will take place that evening. Though the events of the narrative present are not far reaching, the themes and technique employed by Virginia Woolf are nearly limitless. The reader is exposed to Woolf's complex structure as the narrative flows out of the initial action into a memory about Peter Walsh, a man with whom Clarissa had a relationship some thirty years prior. She recalls, in present time reflection, that he will be back from India soon. She has been receiving letters from Peter, and though she finds him dull, she maintains a certain affection for him.

As the narrative proceeds, the reader is made aware that Clarissa Dalloway has suffered through a significant bout of influenza, and though quite pale, she is still attractive. As she makes her way through the park, reveling in her summer surroundings, she runs into her old friend Hugh Whitbread. Hugh tells her that his wife Evelyn is still sick, so he will be attending her party alone. Clarissa proceeds past her old friend and the narrative spirals through a series of connections occurring within her mind, concentrating again on Peter Walsh. The reader is shown the human, hypocritical nature of Clarissa's thoughts as she thinks of the intolerable nature of Peter's possessiveness, while simultaneously experiencing a possessive reaction to his decision, some years ago, to marry an Indian woman. Her thoughts turn to her husband and his ability to act for the sake of action rather than for the sake of influencing outside observers, as Clarissa feels she does. She also feels that her marriage to Richard Dalloway has stripped her of some of her self, going from the independent Clarissa, to Mrs. Richard Dalloway.

Upon reaching Bond Street, where she expects to find the flowers for her party, Clarissa thinks of her daughter Elizabeth and how she does not share her mother's obsession with material goods. Clarissa reflects on her daughter's relationship with the religious fanatic Miss Kilman, by whom Clarissa fears her daughter is too heavily influenced.

Clarissa finally enters Mulberry's flower shop where Miss Pym, the florist, meets her. As they gaze over the assortment of flowers, they are startled by the loud sound coming from an extravagant looking motorcar. Woolf uses this sound as a device to move out of the flower shop and into the street where Septimus Smith, who is sitting on a bench in Regent's park with his Italian wife Lucrezia, also hears the sound.

Septimus jumps off the bench and vows to kill himself. Lucrezia is concerned for her husband and embarrassed that the crowd who gathered can hear his cries by the motorcar. As the couple proceeds into the park, their attention is diverted toward a plane that seems to be writing messages in the sky. Lucrezia encourages her husband to watch the plane as his doctor suggested that he should focus on things outside of himself. It is when Septimus looks up at the plane that the reader is made aware of the extent of his mental illness; he is convinced that the plane is writing secret messages intended only for his eye. His wife walks to the water fountain feeling very distressed. When she returns, Septimus is listening to a bird chirping his name. He gets upset when Lucrezia interrupts.

Woolf uses the spectacle of the plane to shift back into the perspective of Clarissa Dalloway who has just arrived back home. She finds a note on the table and discovers that her husband is eating with Lady Millicent Bruton. Trying not to get upset that she wasn't invited to lunch, Clarissa heads up to her room and lays down. She thinks about her husband and love and how she had once felt a sense of love for her childhood girlfriend Sally Seton. Sally had a magnetic, reckless personality; 'they spoke of marriage always as a catastrophe.' She was the first one who made Clarissa realize how sheltered her life had been growing up in Bourton.

As Clarissa's memory fades back to her husband's lunch with Lady Bruton, she takes her green dress out of the cupboard and holds it before her window, remembering that she had torn it. She decides to mend the dress herself and wear it that evening. Soon after settling onto her seat, the doorbell rings. Peter Walsh enters the house and goes directly upstairs where he surprises Clarissa who had not known exactly when he was returning from India.

With the entrance of Peter, the point of view volleys between Clarissa and Peter. It begins as Peter kisses Clarissa's hands and notices that she appears older. He feels instantly self-conscious about his zealous greeting and takes out his pocketknife, which he has had for as long as Clarissa can remember, and starts to fidget with it. Clarissa recognizes this habit of Peter's and takes notice of his slightly changed appearance. As the conversation continues, both Clarissa and Peter scrutinize each other, each equivalently critical and warm, insecure and nostalgic.

Peter had wanted to marry Clarissa. Likewise, the decision to wed Richard Dalloway had been a difficult one for Clarissa, but the safest decision, and the one that allowed her the greatest sense of independence and security. Peter tells Clarissa of a married woman in India with whom he is in love. Then he breaks into tears. Clarissa kisses his hands and attempts to console him. Peter asks if she is happy in her current life. Before she can answer, Clarissa's daughter Elizabeth interrupts them. Peter greets her and promptly leaves. Clarissa runs after him and reminds him of her party later that evening.

The narrative follows Peter as he exits the Dalloway home and walks toward Regent's Park. He realizes that no one other then Clarissa knows that he has returned to England. He stops beside a statue and sees a young, attractive woman pass. He decides to follow her, walking through several streets until she finally enters into a house. Peter then decides to walk into the park where he finds a bench, sits down, smokes part of a cigar and dozes off.

When he wakes up, he reflects on his days as a young man when he had fallen in love with Clarissa. They had the ability to read each other's thoughts, he believed. And he knew that when she met Richard Dalloway she would marry him. He remembers when their relationship ended; he can still hear himself demanding the truth from Clarissa, and the coldness of her silence.

Peter is taken out of his reflection by the sound of a child who breaks from her nurse and runs into the legs of a woman. The woman is Lucrezia Smith. Woolf takes the reader into the mind of Lucrezia who is distressed over her husband's condition, and upset that she has to suffer because of it. She returns to Septimus and the reader is drawn into the delusional state of his thoughts and perception. Septimus is convinced that he can see through men and into the future, and has witnessed dogs turning into men. He takes these hallucinations as real and searches his mind for a scientific explanation, 'for one must be scientific above all things.'

As Lucrezia walks back to her husband, Septimus witnesses his dead friend Evans approaching. Lucrezia is disturbed by her husband and tries to get him to leave. The reader is made aware that the approaching person, whom Septimus believes to be his dead friend, is in fact Peter Walsh, enchanted at the sight of the arguing couple, likely involved in a lovers' spat. While Peter walks, he reflects on how times have changed since he was a youth. He remembers Sally Seton and how she was ahead of her time, willing to express her opinions without fear of convention. He held considerable respect for her and her ability to see through the shallowness of the British middle-class, in particular Hugh Whitbread. Peter used to take walks with Sally; she would beg him to save Clarissa 'from the Hughs and the Dalloways' of the world.

Peter walks through the park, reflecting on Clarissa and her nature and what his nearly perpetual reflection on her means. He hails a taxi and as he steps into the car, he gives a coin to a homeless woman who is sitting in the gutter. Lucrezia also sees this woman and feels pity. She and her husband are on their way to see another doctor, Sir William Bradshaw.

Lucrezia ruminates on the condition of her husband. Her thoughts are funneled into the narrative and then passed on to a former employer of Septimus', Mr. Brewer. It is through Brewer's reflection that the reader is made aware of Septimus' rise within the military and how initially he had taken the death of his friend Evans quite well. But after the end of the war, when he became engaged to Lucrezia, he began to break down. He lost his ability to feel, believing that the world was without meaning.

Meanwhile, Lucrezia longed desperately for a child. This seemed to push Septimus further into his tormented world of stoicism and existential dread. Dr. Holmes was called to check on him, but insisted that nothing was wrong. Only after Septimus started experiencing auditory hallucinations did Dr. Holmes reluctantly refer him to Sir William Bradshaw. It is here that the narrative resumes present time action. Septimus is seen by Sir William Bradshaw, who is equally as disagreeable, but in a different way. He is arrogant and cold and insists that Septimus should be institutionalized. Lucrezia is turned off by this new doctor who has made her feel even more helpless.

At this point, Woolf passes the narrative baton successively. As Lucrezia is walking, she hears the sound of Big Ben, heard also by Hugh Whitbread. The reader spends a few paragraphs inside Hugh's head, until his thoughts turn to Lady Bruton and her preference for Richard Dalloway. At this point the narrative slant settles at Lady's Bruton's house where Hugh and Richard Dalloway are both lunch guests. Lady Bruton has asked them to her home in hopes of receiving their support and assistance in writing a letter to the *Times* regarding a project relating to Emigration with which she is involved.

After the letter is complete, Richard and Hugh leave Lady Bruton's house. On their way home, they stop at a jewelry store. Though Richard does not really care for Hugh's company, nor for jewelry, he considers buying something for his wife. Not confident that he would choose something tasteful, he decides to leave the store and pick up flowers on his way home. While he's walking he convinces himself that he will tell Clarissa that he loves her, words he hasn't said outright in years. When he does make it home, 'bearing his flowers like a weapon,' he hands them to his wife but does not express his love, feeling too awkward, unnatural.

Clarissa is involved in the preparations for her party. She is torn about whether to invite Ellie Henderson, a woman she feels to be dull. Richard meanwhile convinces himself that he doesn't have to say 'I love you,' to his wife as it's understood. The narrative takes on Clarissa's perspective as she reflects on how she is perceived by others, wondering why she enjoys throwing parties when the excitement could be detrimental to her health. She concludes that she does it all out of a zeal for life.

Clarissa's daughter Elizabeth interrupts her mental meandering to get some gloves. Elizabeth is on her way to the store with Miss Kilman, the religious zealot for whom Clarissa has a sizable distaste. When her daughter leaves, Clarissa reflects on Peter and Miss Kilman and determines that love and religion are the most detestable and destructive things in life.

The narrative moves into the mind of Doris Kilman as she and Elizabeth enter into a cafe. Miss Kilman becomes increasingly paranoid that she is losing her influence on Elizabeth. She tries to conjure up sympathy for herself by speaking of her misfortunes, but this only proves boring and dreary. Eventually Elizabeth gets up to pay the bill and leaves Miss Kilman alone. The narrative follows Elizabeth as she boards an omnibus and heads for the Strand. She acknowledges that she is maturing into womanhood and that she has the opportunity to do anything she chooses with her life.

As Elizabeth returns home, Septimus Smith who is gazing absently out the window of his sitting room sees her bus. Beside him is Lucrezia who is sewing a hat for Mrs. Filmer's married daughter. Septimus slowly starts to converse with his wife. His tone is more normal than it has been in years. Septimus grows increasingly interested in the hat that his wife is sewing. Lucrezia is elated at this semblance of normalcy. They start laughing in excitement and relief. Though Septimus fears that the voices and visions might be waiting around any turn, he allows himself to interact with his wife as he hasn't since they first met.

Then there is a knock at the door. It's the small girl who brings the evening paper. While Septimus is alone, his mind gets more paranoid and tangled. When his wife comes back he is tense. Then Dr. Holmes comes to the door. Lucrezia tries to prevent him from entering the house, as she doesn't want him to disturb her husband's current state, but he makes it past her. Septimus decides that instead of facing the scrutiny of the doctor, he will commit suicide. He searches for options and concludes that the window is the only one. When Dr. Holmes enters the room, Septimus says 'I'll give it you!' and leaps out the window.

As the ambulance races to the hospital with Septimus' mangled body, its sound is heard by Peter Walsh who is walking back to his hotel. While he walks he thinks of Clarissa Dalloway and the impact she has had on his life. When he gets to his hotel, there is a letter from her. It reads simply that she was delighted to see him. He gets mildly upset at the brief letter which she must have written and sent immediately for it to have arrived so soon. His mind wanders to Daisy, the woman whom he hopes to marry upon his return to India. She is only twenty-four and has two small children. Peter takes his reflection down to the hotel restaurant where he eats and decides that he will attend Clarissa's party.

After his dinner, Peter walks to the Dalloway's home. His presence is announced at the door. He is met by Clarissa who expresses delight. Peter cringes at what he perceives to be insincerity. Clarissa suspects that Peter is critical of her, and worries that her party will be a failure.

The party proceeds and the reader is given an outsider's perspective through the lens of Ellie Henderson whom Clarissa invited at the last minute. While making her social rounds, Clarissa is surprised at the sight of her childhood friend, Sally Seton. Sally happened to be in town and had heard about the party. She tells Clarissa that she is married with five sons. But just as they get talking, Clarissa is whisked away to greet the Prime Minister, one of her more distinguished guests.

Clarissa and the Prime Minister are seen by Peter Walsh who makes a mental note of the elitist nature of these parties. The narrative stays with Peter while he watches Clarissa mingle. Eventually he is lead by Clarissa to her Aunt Helena who had written a book on Burma some years ago. Clarissa then goes over to Lady Bruton who mentions how helpful Richard was earlier that afternoon.

Sally spots Peter and they immediately engage in conversation. Meanwhile, Clarissa greets Sir William Bradshaw and his wife who tell her of the unfortunate incident that had taken place earlier in the afternoon. They describe how a young man who had been in the army (Septimus) had killed himself. 'Oh! thought Clarissa, in the middle of my party, here's death, she thought.'

Clarissa grows increasingly upset by the Bradshaws' insistent discussion of this young man's death. Her mind tangents about the inevitability of death, and what it all means. She notes the fragility of life. 'She felt somehow very like him—the young man who had killed himself. She felt glad that he had done it; thrown it away . . . He made her feel the beauty; made her feel the fun.'

The narrative turns to the conversation between Sally and Peter. They are speaking of their lives and discussing old times. Their focus turns to the people at the party as they file out of the Dalloway's home. Peter and Sally admire Elizabeth Dalloway, standing by her father. Sally gets up to wish Richard good night, never having spoken at length with Clarissa. The novel ends as Peter feels a sudden sense of excitement, realizing that the source of this excitement is Clarissa herself, who is standing directly before him. ❁

# List of Characters in
## *Mrs. Dalloway*

**Clarissa Dalloway** is the heroine of the novel and the first character the reader encounters. The present time events of the novel lead up to the dinner party that she has planned. The narrative tracks her struggles with love and relationships, as well as her existential anxieties.

**Richard Dalloway** is Clarissa's husband. He is a well-respected and stable individual who is a Member of Parliament. It is his stability that attracts Clarissa to him. He has difficulty expressing his affection for her.

**Peter Walsh** fell in love with Clarissa when they were young. They were fostering a relationship before she met Richard Dalloway. Peter lived for an extended period in India. He returned to England, from India, on the day that the novel takes place.

**Septimus Warren Smith** is a young man who returned from the war with sever mental trauma. He spends most of the novel lost in hallucination before he finally kills himself.

**Lucrezia Smith** is Septimus' wife. She wants desperately to find help for her husband.

**Hugh Whitbread** is a snobby, but fairly well respected editorialist and government worker. He has lunch at Lady Bruton's house with Richard Dalloway.

**Lady Millicent Bruton** is a member of high society with an interest in government. She hosts Richard and Hugh for lunch so they will help her write a letter highlighting one of her political projects.

**Doris Kilman** is a religious zealot who tries to spread her influence over Clarissa's daughter Elizabeth.

**Elizabeth Dalloway** is Clarissa and Richard's daughter.

**Dr. Holmes** is the first doctor who attempts to treat Septimus. He is characterized as stubborn and egotistical.

**Sir William Bradshaw** is a medical specialist who also tries to treat Septimus. He is also characterized as stubborn and egotistical.

**Sally Seton/Lady Rosseter** is an old friend of Clarissa's who was once rebellious and now has a husband and five sons. She represents Clarissa's true but unfulfilled love. ❀

# Critical Views on
## *Mrs. Dalloway*

[Allen McLaurin has been a teacher, critic and essayist. His works include *Virginia Woolf: The Echoes Enslaved*. In this excerpt, McLaurin speaks on the mock-epic element in the novel.]

The mock-epic element in *Mrs Dalloway* has often been compared with Joyce's use of epic in *Ulysses*. It is evident how much more general are Virginia Woolf's allusions. Her framework is not a particular epic, but, as I have tried to establish, a keyboard of symbols. She is much more concerned with the general type of simile or theme in epic poetry, and particularly with the glorification of war which led to the sickening waste of the First World War. This waste and degradation is conveyed in the irony of the allusion to Ceres in the following passage:

> Something was up, Mr Brewer knew; Mr Brewer, managing clerk at Sibley's and Arrowsmith's, auctioneers, valuers, land and estate agents; something was up, he thought, and, being paternal with his young men, and thinking very highly of Smith's abilities, and prophesying that he would, in ten or fifteen years, succeed to the leather arm-chair in the inner room under the skylight with the deed-boxes around him, 'if he keeps his health,' said Mr Brewer, and that was the danger—he looked weakly; advised football, invited him to supper and was seeing his way to consider recommending a rise of salary, when something happened which threw out many of Mr Brewer's calculations, took away his ablest young fellows, and eventually, so prying and insidious were the fingers of the European War, smashed the plaster cast of Ceres, ploughed a hole in the geranium beds, and utterly ruined the cook's nerves at Mr Brewer's establishment at Muswell Hill.

The gods and heroes of the novel are made of plaster. Hugh Whitbread is not 'the stout-hearted', he is 'the admirable', and his role is simply that of a sycophant at court. 'By Jove' is simply a mild expression of surprise: 'How they loved dressing up in gold lace and doing homage! There! That must be—by Jove it was—Hugh Whitbread, snuffing round the precincts of the great, grown rather fatter, rather whiter, the admirable Hugh!' The threefold repetition of a name a little earlier establishes the mock-heroic undertone of these pages:

> But alas, Wilkins; Wilkins wanted her; Wilkins was emitting in a voice of commanding authority, as if the whole company must be admonished and the hostess reclaimed from frivolity, one name:
> 'The Prime Minister,' said Peter Walsh.

The military aspect of the epic is never forgotten. For example, Clarissa's parasol is seen as the sacred weapon of a goddess and Richard Dalloway comes 'bearing his flowers like a weapon'. The general ironic light of the novel plays over the symbols of public life:

> As for Buckingham Palace (like an old prima donna facing the audience all in white) you can't deny it a certain dignity, he considered, nor despise what does, after all, stand to millions of people (a little crowd was waiting at the gate to see the King drive out) for a symbol, absurd though it is; a child with a box of bricks could have done better, he thought; looking at the memorial to Queen Victoria (whom he could remember in her horn spectacles driving through Kensington), its white mound, its billowing motherliness; but he liked being ruled by the descendant of Horsa; he liked continuity; and the sense of handing on the traditions of the past.

Scientific, religious, and heroic faiths have been smashed by the First World War. The cross, the aeroplane, the monument of Queen Victoria are no longer acceptable whole-heartedly, for they no longer bring human beings together. All that Clarissa Dalloway can do is literally bring them together at a party, so that for one moment they feel their common humanity. This is itself only a symbolic gesture, a greeting to other beings across the emptiness which she sees at the heart of life. Septimus is there only in spirit, and represents all that has been lost in the War. The news of his death puts Clarissa's party into a classical setting, with the theme of 'Et in Arcadia Ego', and in an undertone is the Anglican Service for the Burial of the Dead:

Oh! Thought Clarissa, in the middle of my party, here's
death, she thought.

—Allen McLaurin, *Virginia Woolf: The Echoes Enslaved* (Cambridge,
Cambridge University Press, 1973): pp. 156–157.

## MANLY JOHNSON ON *MRS. DALLOWAY*

[Manly Johnson has been a professor of English at the university of Tulsa. She has taught extensive seminars of Virginia Woolf and her work. In this excerpt, Johnson speaks
on the dominating tendency of certain characters in the
novel, and its subsequent effect.]

Virginia Woolf exposes relentlessly the mania to dominate of people
like Lady Bruton, Sir William, and Dr. Holmes. The clinical madness
of Septimus is represented as a consequence in their manipula-
tions—indirectly, as in the case of Lady Bruton's political and social
schemes, and directly in the perverted "healing" of Bradshaw and
Holmes.

Septimus is the victim of a war-induced neurosis. Having volun-
teered early in the war of 1914–18, he suffered for four years the
frustration of his idealistic impulse to "save England for Shakespeare." Withstanding the successive traumas of combat, he is
stricken by the survivor's guilt after his friend Evans is killed. Crip-
pled within, he seeks out Lucrezia to marry her, with the instinctive
knowledge that her health is what his sickness needs. She appears to
him as the tree of life,

> as if all her petals were about her. She was a flowering tree;
> and through her branches looked out the face of a law-giver,
> who had reached a sanctuary where she feared no one.

His instinct was right and she is good for him, but because she is
inexperienced and a foreigner, she is not capable of protecting him
against the malpractices, condoned by society, of such "healers" as
Holmes and Sir William.

Sir William, a large distinguished-looking man, would not appear to be insane in any clinical sense. But he makes everyone profoundly uneasy in his presence. He is a self-made man, we discover, who has permitted himself to be shaped by the materialistic values that reward domination. In treating his patients he invoked all the forces of society to gain their submission. "Naked, defenseless, the exhausted, the friendless received the impress of Sir William's will. He swooped; he devoured. He shut people up." In his compulsion to put people away, Woolf casts Sir William as an agent of death. For insanity, as she describes it, is isolation from people, from things, from all the stuff of life—death, in short.

> —Manly Johnson, *Virginia Woolf* (New York, Frederick Ungar Publishing Co., 1973): pp. 61–62.

## MITCHELL A. LEASKA ON *MRS. DALLOWAY*

[Mitchell A. Leaska has been a professor of English at Brooklyn College and New York University. He has published several books including *The Voice of Tragedy, Virginia Woolf's Lighthouse: A Study in Critical Method* and *The Novels of Virginia Woolf: From Beginning to End.* In this excerpt, Leaska speaks on the many layers of the novel.]

"For there she was." So ends Virginia Woolf's fourth novel; and upon these four words rests the full weight of its meaning. Exactly how we interpret them depends upon how we have read all the preceding pages; whether we have caught in this novel's seamless world of psychology and doubt the minute signals strewn everywhere, the small half visible evasions and turns which have the shaping power of invention and suggestion; whether we have heard those near inaudible sounds and repetitions of word and phrase which collect and build an edifice of feeling so infallibly arranged and welded together; whether we have glimpsed the shadow play of consciousness and motive so abysmal with ambiguity and possibility as to make critical commentary appear to reside in some ablative region on the far side of language.

"As the publishers frankly say," wrote the reviewer, D.R., "'this novel does not belong to the multitude.' The Galsworthy refinement will not always be understood, nor are all readers proficient in the difficult gymnastic of jumping in and out of other people's skins. But it is a book which will be highly praised by the sensitive minority." Joseph Wood Krutch who interpreted the novel through Clarissa, who to him "seems to assure those who come near her that life, even though it have neither harmony nor meaning, may yet be lived with a certain comeliness if one does not ask too much of it; and thus Mrs. Woolf reinvestigates a very old sort of loveliness." Another reviewer found a "resentfulness" in Clarissa, "some paucity of spiritual graces, or rather some positive hideousness." Having admired Mrs. Woolf's prose and compared her with her contemporaries, he returns to the novel through Clarissa: her impression, her memories, "the events which are initiated remotely and engineered almost to touching distance of the impervious Clarissa, capture in a definitive matrix the drift of thought and feeling in a period, the point of view of a class, and seem almost to indicate the strength and weakness of an entire civilization."

Some of the entries Virginia Woolf made in her *Diary* during the revision of *Mrs. Dalloway* lead us to suspect that she knew many of her reviewers would not understand the intricacy of her design and would miss the connections between Clarissa and Septimus. She was right. Probably because she thought her readers would not understand its design, she wrote a preface to the novel when it was to be reprinted in 1928. In it she provided an important clue to the novel's form and meaning:

> To tell the reader anything that his own imagination and insight have not already discovered would need not a page or two of preface but a volume or two of autobiography. . . . Of *Mrs. Dalloway* then one can only bring to light at the moment a few scraps, of little importance or none perhaps; as that in the first version Septimus, who later is intended to be her double, had no existence; and that Mrs. Dalloway was originally to kill herself or perhaps merely to die at the end of the party.

This statement quite naturally generated a whirlwind of new readings of the novel, but the question of *how* Septimus is Clarissa's double has remained a stony and stubborn riddle. As Keith Hollingworth wrote: "The clue, nevertheless, remains a puzzle in itself: when the differences between Septimus and Clarissa bulk larger than the likenesses, how can he be her double?" The answer to that is not easy, but to get at part of it requires our understanding something of Mrs. Woolf's method in order to see how the *personae* are aligned in relation to one another.

—Mitchell A. Leaska, T*he Novels of Virginia Woolf: From Beginning to End* (New York, The John Jay Press, 1977): pp. 85–86.

## HOWARD HARPER ON *MRS. DALLOWAY*

[Howard Harper has been a professor of English at the University of North Carolina. He is the author of *Desperate Faith*, a study of Bellow, Mailer, Salinger, Baldwin and Updike. In this excerpt, Harper speaks on the mysterious world of Bourton.]

Now, many years later, Bourton remains a mysterious world which in some ways Clarissa, despite her obsession with it, does not wish to think about. There is one striking passage, for example, in which Peter thinks about Clarissa's skepticism:

> her notion being that the Gods, who never lost a chance of hurting, thwarting and spoiling human lives, were seriously put out if, all the same, you behaved like a lady. That phase came directly after Sylvia's death—that horrible affair. To see your own sister killed by a falling tree (all Justin Parry's fault—all his carelessness) before your very eyes, a girl too on the verge of life, the most gifted of them, Clarissa always said, was enough to turn one bitter. Later . . . she evolved his atheist's religion of doing good for the sake of goodness.

It seems strange that Clarissa herself never thinks of Sylvia's death, even though she does think of her father several times during this day. What she had said about it to Peter must have led to his feeling that it was all her father's fault, and that she later came to believe that "no one was to blame." Did she really believe that? or did she repress her earlier feeling? Her comment that Sylvia was "the most gifted of them" may imply that to be gifted is to be doomed—and could help to explain Clarissa's own reluctance to appear to be different. Unconsciously, she—and the narrative—might feel somehow that Sylvia's fate is that of the "gifted girl," and even that the father may be implicated in that fate.

While we can only speculate about Clarissa's complicated feelings about her father and about her sister's death, we can see more clearly the repressive nature of Bourton. "Sally it was who made her feel, for the first time, how sheltered the life at Bourton was," Clarissa thinks—Sally, who read William Morris, sat up all night talking, smoked cigars, rode a bicycle around the parapets of the terrace, forgot her bath sponge and ran naked down a corridor—for which she was summoned into the commanding presence of Helena Parry. The household had been governed by Aunt Helena (a more elderly Helen Ambrose?), aided by such stalwarts as the "grim old housemaid, Ellen Atkins," entertained by such guests as "old Joseph Breitkopf singing Brahms without any voice," and presided over by the figure whom Peter remembers as "that querulous, weak-kneed old man, Clarissa's father, Justin Parry" (a geriatric evolution of Ridley Ambrose and Mr. Hilbery).

Conspicuously absent from all of this is the mother. Until Mrs. Hilbery mentions her at Clarissa's party, she exists only by implication and indirection and, in one strange moment in Clarissa's mind during Peter's visit: then Clarissa becomes both "a child, throwing bread to the ducks, between her parents, and at the same time a grown woman coming to her parents who stood by the lake," holding out her life for their inspection. What has she made of their gift of life? she wonders—another sign of the pall of guilt which hangs over her. Old Mrs. Hilbery, of course, is a more elderly version of the mother in *Night and Day*. It is she who mentions Clarissa's mother for the only time in *Mrs. Dalloway*:

> "Dear Clarissa!" exclaimed Mrs. Hilbery. She looked tonight, she said, so like her mother as she first saw her walking in a garden in a grey hat.
> And really Clarissa's eyes filled with tears. Her mother, walking in a garden! But alas, she must go.

> —Howard Harper, *Between Language and Silence: The Novels of Virginia Woolf* (Baton Rouge, Louisiana State University Press, 1982): pp. 113–115.

## Judy Little on Myth and Manner in the Early Novels

> [Judy Little has been a professor of English at Southern Illinois University, Carbondale. She is the author of *Keats as a Narrative Poet: A Test of Invention*. In this excerpt, Little speaks on the mystery that Clarissa Dalloway sees at the heart of every person.]

Like the narrator of *Jacob's Room*, Clarissa Dalloway is convinced that there is a mystery at the heart of each person. She is amused, and sometimes angered, if anyone tries "forcing" the "soul," tries to fasten down a rigid destructive definition of "human nature." By many critics, Clarissa would not be considered a trustworthy judge of human beings; she is seen as cold, sexless, and artificial, an empty-headed socialite. But Virginia Woolf, and Clarissa as well, seem to agree with the critics about the limitations of the major character's sensibility. After finishing *Mrs. Dalloway* (1925), Woolf was concerned that Clarissa might be "too glittering and tinsely." Clarissa and her social world are themselves one of the objects of satire in the novel. Woolf wrote that she hoped to "criticise the social system," a phrase that could mean either the criticism of the artificial life of society people in general, or, as Alex Zwerdling argues, the criticism of the stoical postwar upper-class attitude which takes care to exclude sensitive outsiders like the suicide Septimus Smith. Woolf's attitude toward the society women of her acquaintance, such as Kitty Maxse and Lady Ottoline Morrell, was ambiguous, and something of this ambiguity is present in Clarissa's character.

Clarissa is troubled by the compromises she has made in her life. During the time span of the novel's surface "plot," the day in which Clarissa prepares for her party that evening, she thinks of ten of her past decisions and of her present life as hostess, an obligatory role for the wife of Richard Dalloway, M.P. She recognizes that her marriage to Richard and her constant social life have perhaps tarnished her heart; something has been "defaced, obscured in her own life, let drop every day in corruption, lies, chatter." And yet Clarissa does recognize the value of what she has preserved, salvaged from people like the psychiatrist Sir William Bradshaw, a man capable of "forcing your soul," whose inept, insensitive response contributed much to the death of Septimus. Clarissa knows that she still retains the energy and happiness of her love for her girlhood friend Sally Seton (who has succumbed to egotistical motherhood), and Clarissa recognizes also that her friendly marriage to Richard has preserved her privacy and independence, her "self-respect—something, after all, priceless." The lies and corruption of her decision to marry Richard, though she loved Peter Walsh, have given her in compensation the continuing opportunity to bring people together in her parties, her "offering" to life, given "for no reason whatever," an "offering for the sake of offering, perhaps." Her parties, as one critic has observed, are an expression of creative artistry, a courageous celebration poised against war and against intrusive people, including Peter and the zealous Miss Kilman, who try to force the soul into a tight mold. Clarissa's party, which is the focus and culmination of the novel's action, occurs as a gesture of celebration and communication in a society that tends to confine people to narrow and discrete psychological boxes. Jacob pretty well escaped the stereotypes with which his education would have restricted him; he escaped by ignoring the classic growth pattern for respectable young men. All of the characters in *Mrs. Dalloway*, however, have compromised to some extent with the culture that defines them. More than the others, Clarissa has retained the "treasure" of a private self, as recent critics are careful to emphasize.

—Judy Little, *Comedy and the Woman Writer: Woolf, Spark, and Feminism* (Lincoln, University of Nebraska Press, 1983): pp. 48–49.

## EMILY JENSEN ON CLARISSA DALLOWAY'S RESPECTABLE SUICIDE

[Emily Jensen has been the head of the English Department at Lycoming College, Williamsport, Penn. She has published several essays, as well as a critical volume on women writers and suicide. In this excerpt, Jensen speaks on the dichotomies in Clarissa Dalloway's life.]

The novel begins with an image that initiates a number of verbal strains, each of which is played upon later on:

What a lark! What a plunge! For so it had always seemed to her, when, with a little squeak of the hinges, which she could hear now, she had burst open the French windows and plunged at Bourton into the open air. How fresh, how calm, stiller than this of course, the air was in the early morning; like the flap of a wave; the kiss of a wave; chill and sharp and yet (for a girl of eighteen as she then was) solemn, feeling as she did, standing there at the open window, that something awful was about to happen.

"Plunge . . . Bourton . . . this . . . solemn . . . ; something awful was about to happen." Thus, on the first page of the novel, the dichotomies in Clarissa's life are established: "Bourton" versus "this" and "plunging" into life versus the "solemn" fear "that something awful was about to happen." That Bourton represents both Sally and Clarissa's love for women becomes clear in the extended memory sequence occasioned by Clarissa's discovery that Lady Bruton had asked Richard to lunch without her; that fact "made the moment in which she stood shiver," recalling to her mind other moments. First she recalls her many failures with Richard, but then her moments of success with women, when "for that moment, she had seen an illumination, a match burning in a crocus; an inner meaning almost expressed." Woolf insists that we perceive Clarissa's awareness that it is with women that she has experienced her most intense moments of passion by telling us so outright: "It was over—the moment. Against such moments (with women too) there contrasted (as she laid her hat down) the bed." Of course it is Clarissa's need also not quite to see what she sees—"an inner meaning almost expressed"— for, as will become clear later, she spends a good deal of her time attempting to justify to herself having chosen "the bed" of her current life over those intense moments. In either case, whether for the reader's benefit or Clarissa's, it is superfluous to say "with women too," since the entire passage concerns women; it is, in fact, inaccurate, since men are not included at all.

But this question of love (she thought, putting her coat away), this falling in love with women. Take Sally Seton; her relation in the old days with Sally Seton. Had not that, after all, been love?

Certainly the intensity of the lengthy passage that follows can leave no doubt in our minds or in Clarissa's as to the nature of her feelings for Sally Seton: "But all that evening she could not take her eyes off Sally. . . . Sally it was who made her feel, for the first time, how sheltered her life at Bourton was. She knew nothing about sex—nothing about social problems. . . . She could remember standing in her bedroom at the top of the house holding the hot water can in her hands and saying aloud, 'she is beneath this roof . . . she is beneath this roof!'" Hot water can, indeed. For despite Clarissa's disclaimer that the words carry no meaning for her anymore, doing her hair in the present does begin to bring back the old feeling:

> "if it were now to die 'twere now to be most happy." That was her feeling—Othello's feeling, and she felt it, she was convinced, as strongly as Shakespeare meant Othello to feel it, all because she was coming down to dinner in a white frock to meet Sally Seton!

It is neither insignificant nor unrelated (as very little is in this novel of delicate weavings, tiny stitches overlaying other stitches to form a textured pattern) that Septimus Smith survives the war and the loss of his friend Evans to discover that he has lost the ability to feel; in his case, as in Clarissa's, the feeling that is lost is for a person of his own sex. Nor is it unrelated that both of them call upon Shakespeare: while Clarissa identifies with Othello's passion for Desdemona, Septimus focuses on the meaning behind Shakespeare's words, that "love between man and woman was repulsive." Taken together, these allusions give us the quality of the feeling subsequently lost and the homosexual nature of it.

—Emily Jensen, "Clarissa Dalloway's Respectable Suicide" in *Virginia Woolf: A Feminist Slant,* Jane Marcus, ed. (Lincoln, University of Nebraska Press, 1983): pp. 163–164.

# Plot Summary of
## *To the Lighthouse*

*To the Lighthouse,* considered by many to be Virginia Woolf's most accomplished novel, utilizes many of the personalities and landscapes from Woolf's own childhood. It is set in three parts, spanning over ten years. The **first part**, 'The Window', opens at the Ramsay's summer home as Mrs. Ramsay tells her son James that if it is nice in the morning, they will go to the lighthouse. James, who is busy cutting out pictures in a catalog, is overjoyed at the prospect of a voyage. But his joy is quickly severed by his father's insistence that it will be too wet to go to the lighthouse. 'Had there been an axe handy, or a poker, any weapon that would have gashed a hole in his father's breast and killed him, there and then, James would have seized it.' The reader is told how Mr. Ramsay's mere presence has the power to stir an extreme range of emotions within people, particularly his children. Consistent with many of her other novels, *To the Lighthouse* captures multiple points of view. The reader is confronted with this structure early in the novel as the narrative tells of the thoughts that pass through James' brain before moving deftly on to Mrs. Ramsay who is trying to salvage some of the hope that was stolen from her little boy.

Charles Tansley, a student of philosophy who holds Mr. Ramsay in high regard, adds to the fray by mentioning that the winds are blowing away from the lighthouse. Though Mrs. Ramsay is upset that Tansley has added unnecessarily to her son's distress, she notes how her children have ridiculed him—often calling him 'the atheist'—and refrains from holding a grudge. Woolf indulges the reader with a description of Mrs. Ramsay's good nature and her high regard for guests, particularly male, before cutting right back to Charles Tansley as he repeats that there will be no traveling to the lighthouse.

Before long, the children and the other guests leave with Mr. Ramsay, and Mrs. Ramsay asks Charles to join her on an errand in town. Before leaving, they pass Augustus Carmichael and ask if he needs anything. He says he doesn't and as they walk by, Mrs. Ramsay tells Tansley that Carmichael could have been a gifted philosopher were it not for an unfortunate marriage. Charles appreciates hearing this gossip, as he has often felt snubbed by the other members of the Ramsay family.

On the walk, Charles grows increasingly comfortable, talking with greater ease about his life and his ambitions. Though Mrs. Ramsay finds his tales boring, she indulges her guest for the sake of his comfort. They finally stop at a house where Mrs. Ramsay spends a few minutes upstairs attending to business. When she returns, Charles has convinced himself that she is the most beautiful person he has ever met.

In the ensuing section, still within the first part, the narrative returns to the discussion of the lighthouse. Mrs. Ramsay assures her son that a trip to the lighthouse is not entirely out of the question. She remembers that she is supposed to remain still for Lily Briscoe who is painting a picture of the landscape, including the window where she is sitting with James.

The narrative moves to Lily Briscoe, in the process of capturing the house and landscape around her. She is approached by William Bankes, who lodges in the same housing village. The reader is told of the relationship that William Bankes once had with Mr. Ramsay and how it had grown stale. But despite their distance, Bankes still holds him in high regard and has a great deal of respect for his accomplishments. It is through Lily and William's conversation that the reader is filled in about Mr. Ramsay's accomplishments and the subsequent plateau that he reached following his early success. 'He had made a definite contribution to philosophy in one little book when he was only five and twenty; what came after was more or less amplification, repetition.' The fair-minded Bankes makes a point to acknowledge that the 'number of men who make a definite contribution to anything whatsoever is very small,' thus his respect for Ramsay. Lily, who is prone to deep shifts in emotion, is very taken by Bankes' point of view, feeling tremendous respect for his seemingly unbiased perspective. Ironically, their conversation is interrupted by Mr. Ramsay who appears infuriated.

The narrative picks up again inside where Mrs. Ramsay continues to console her son, assuring him that there will be other days to go to the lighthouse. She is in the process of knitting a stocking for Mr. Sorley's boy, using James as a model. Her mind roams to the time of her father's death and how beautiful the mountains had appeared at that time.

Meanwhile, Mr. Ramsay, still ranting about an ambiguous blunder, starts to obsess over his status in the philosophical world.

He imagines accomplishments on an alphabetical scale, where he has been able to reach a respectable Q, though unable to move beyond it. 'In that flash of darkness he heard people saying—he was a failure—that R was beyond him.' He muses further about how, and if, he will be remembered after he's gone, rationalizing this shallow reflection as reasonable, if not inevitable given human curiosity.

Mr. Ramsay approaches his wife and insists that he is a failure. Mrs. Ramsay does her best to reassure her husband, reminding him of what people like Charles Tansley are always saying of him. Eventually he walks off leaving Mrs. Ramsay unsettled by her husband's vulnerability. Following a circuitous narrative route through the mind of Mrs. Ramsay, the narrative settles again within the head of Mr. Ramsay as he determines that 'he inspired in William Bankes (intermittently) and in Charles Tansley (obsequiously) and in his wife . . . reverence, and pity, and gratitude too.'

Meanwhile, the narrative turns to Lily Briscoe whose mind is wandering during a conversation with William Bankes. She comes out of her reflection when she realizes that Bankes has put on his glasses and is now looking at her painting. Though she feels vulnerable and insecure, she decides to embrace the opportunity to share her work with another person. Bankes asks about a purple triangle that he can't quite decipher. Lily answers that it is meant to be Mrs. Ramsay reading to James in the window, and even though it bears no exact likeness, it is part of the entire landscape that deals which the balance of light and dark and the necessary connections between objects.

Inside the house, Mrs. Ramsay continues to read the story of the Fisherman and His Wife to James, while simultaneously indulging thoughts of acquaintances, one of whom "had once accused her of 'robbing her of her daughter's affections.'" One of the few blemishes in the perception of Mrs. Ramsay exists in her tendency to control situations, 'to interfere, making people do what she wished.'

As Mrs. Ramsay reflects on the complexities of life, her husband strolls into the room and before long, they engage in conversation. They walk out on the terrace, both seeming to know what the other is thinking. Their mental meanderings tread on melancholy trails, where worry and regret consistently rear their heads. Despite the nature of their reflections, they convince themselves that they have a lot to be happy about, as they have eight children, all of whom seem to be headed in a positive direction. As they gaze out to their yard, they see Lily Briscoe and William Bankes walking together. Mrs. Ramsay hopes that their walk is a step toward marriage.

Meanwhile, Minta Doyle, a friend of the Ramsays, and Paul Rayley, Minta's boyfriend are walking to the beach with Nancy and Andrew, two of the Ramsays' children. The narrative floats through Nancy's mind as she sees Minta and Paul kissing by the water. Their moment is broken, however, when Minta realizes that she has lost the brooch that her grandmother had given her. Paul searches for the brooch until it becomes too dark and they decide to return to the Ramsay's house. As they walk, the reader is made aware that Minta and Paul are now engaged.

The next scene takes place in the dining room where Mrs. Ramsay has invited several guests to dinner. She assigns everyone a seat and takes her place at the head of the table, opposite her husband.

In true Virginia Woolf style, the narrative floats through many perspectives throughout the coarse of the meal. Early on, the reader is privy to the thoughts of Lily Briscoe who is thinking about her painting and her dislike of Charles Tansley. Despite her dislike for him, Lily feels obliged to engage him in pleasant conversation. 'She had done the usual trick—been nice. She would never know him. He would never know her. Human relations were all like that, she thought, and the worst (if it had not been for Mr. Bankes) were between men and women. Inevitably these were extremely insincere she thought.'

After the soup has been cleared, candles are lit and Minta and Paul finally arrive. Mrs. Ramsay suspects instantly that they are engaged. Despite Minta declaring that she lost her grandmother's brooch, there is a perceptible glow in her face. Just after their arrival, the dinner, *boeuf en daube*, a French recipe passed down from Mrs. Ramsay's grandmother, is served. Mrs. Ramsay makes a point to give William Bankes the most tender piece. He finds the dish exquisite and makes a point to tell his host how pleased he is. At the end of the meal, Augustus Carmichael recites a poem and bows graciously toward Mrs. Ramsay.

The Ramsay's guests take leave of the table and convene both out on the terrace and inside the living room. Mrs. Ramsay goes upstairs to check on Cam and James, discovering that they are still awake.

Cam cannot sleep because she is afraid of the pig skull that is hanging on the wall. James refuses to let anyone take it down. Mrs. Ramsay tries to please all by wrapping her green shawl around it, concealing its shape. Sensing that her children are satisfied, she heads back downstairs, assuring James that they will travel to the lighthouse as soon as the weather allows.

When she gets downstairs, Mr. Ramsay meets Minta and Paul who are going outside to look at the waves. Mrs. Ramsay feels excited and youthful as the young couple leaves. She walks into the other room where her husband is reading a book by Sir Walter Scott, whom he greatly admires. Mrs. Ramsay picks up her knitting and reflects on her husband. She eventually swaps her knitting for a book of poetry.

Mr. Ramsay finishes a chapter from the Scott book and feels deeply moved. After reflecting on the situations in the chapter, he gazes at his wife and is pleased by how peaceful she appears. Mrs. Ramsay senses her husband's gaze and puts down her book. Pressured for something to say, she tells her husband that Minta and Paul are engaged. Mr. Ramsay thinks about how difficult it is for his wife to express her love aloud. Sensing her husband's desire for amorous expression, Mrs. Ramsay, incapable of stating her love outright, concedes that he was right about the weather not being suitable for the lighthouse. 'For she had triumphed again. She had not said it: yet he knew.'

In **Part II,** 'Time Passes', Woolf opens with a new narrative mode. While Part I is filled with the hyperconscious minds of multiple characters, allowing single moments to stretch out for pages, the narrative in Part II concentrates more on external details rather than jockeying internal reflection. The reader is told that many nights have passed, and then, in the belly of brackets, that Mrs. Ramsay has died. And it is in brackets where the narrative reveals how Prue married, ['how beautiful she looked!'] and later died ['in some illness related to childbirth.'] Then further on: ['A Shell exploded. Twenty or thirty young men were blown up in France, among them Andrew Ramsay, whose death, mercifully, was instantaneous.']

Woolf presents a tremendous contrast from the weighted reflections of Part I, where trivial matters were treated with painful intensity, to the brackets in Part II where monumental events are presented as inconsequential asides. The final bracket in this particular section of Part II mentions that Augustus Carmichael had published a widely successful volume of poetry, suggesting that the war had revived the public's interest in poetry.

During the ten years since Part I, the Ramsay's house is all but abandoned. Mrs. McNab, the elderly housekeeper, allows the house to deteriorate. But when she receives a letter indicating that Mr. Ramsay, Cam, James, Nancy and Jasper, as well as Lily Briscoe and Augustus Carmichael will be returning to the house for a visit, she does her best to get the house back in order. Part II ends as Lily Briscoe and Augustus Carmichael return to the house and settle down for the night.

**Part III,** 'The Lighthouse', opens in the morning as Lily Briscoe, who had arrived the previous night, attempts to come to terms with the fact that she is once again inside the Ramsay's house and Mrs. Ramsay is no longer alive. Lily engages in existential reflection regarding the chaotic relationship between objects and events. She decides to resume her work on the painting she had abandoned nearly ten years ago, hoping it will help gel the chaotic forces that swirl inside her.

Meanwhile, Mr. Ramsay, Cam and James arrive by boat to their house. They have plans to travel to the lighthouse the following morning. In a brief, awkward conversation between Lily and Mr. Ramsay, it becomes clear that Woolf has returned to the narrative mode that dominated Part I, as the reader is made aware of the hyper reflections that consume their minds, both yearning for the stability which they associate with the late Mrs. Ramsay.

The following morning, James, Cam and Mr. Ramsay set out by boat to the lighthouse with an acquaintance named Macalister and his son. On route, Mr. Ramsay encourages Mr. Macalister to tell him about a winter storm which he had experienced. As they head away from the house, Mr. Ramsay tells his children to look at their house in the distance. Cam does not actively respond and her father teases her. The narrative follows Cam's thoughts, viewing her father as a tyrant and her brother as a hero, with the strength to captain the boat and stand up for himself.

The narrative turns back to Lily Briscoe who is painting and musing about the past. She thinks of Paul and Minta and imagines that their marriage was not successful, conjuring up fictionalized scenarios in which there is considerable tension. She thinks about

William Bankes and how she had resisted marrying him, despite her great admiration and respect for him. Her fantasies all circle back to Mrs. Ramsay, whose influence is still very much alive within Lily. 'The whole world seemed to have dissolved in this early morning hour into a pool of thought, a deep basin of reality.' This section ends with Lily crying out for Mrs. Ramsay.

The next section consists of a two-sentence bracket about the fish caught and released by Macalister's boy, before returning again to Lily Briscoe, who is still crying for Mrs. Ramsay. The narrative notes the anguish and existential anxiety that periodically consumes Lily, particularly now that she is confronted by old memories and the passing of time.

The narrative resumes inside James' mind as their boat makes its way to the lighthouse. James is consumed by the presence and influence of his father, for whom he maintains a tangible disregard. He remembers how upset he had been ten years earlier when his father had insisted that it would be too wet to travel to the lighthouse. He remembers how he had wanted to drive a knife into his father's heart. He imagines doing the same thing now. Meanwhile, Cam, who is also reflecting on the domineering, often egotistical nature of her father, has found something endearing in the manner by which he is relaxing on the boat, his legs curled and his eyes pinned to the pages of a book.

Lily Briscoe, still in the process of painting, is musing about Augustus Carmichael who is sleeping on the grass near where she is painting. She imagines that she knows what his poems are about, despite having never read them.

Meanwhile, Mr. Ramsay finally puts down his book and suggests that they all eat lunch. Then he looks at his watch, acknowledges the vicinity to the lighthouse and expresses his satisfaction at having made good time. James, who is captaining the boat, is elated by his father's compliment.

When they finally arrive at the lighthouse, the narrative moves back to the perspective of Lily Briscoe. She says she believes the boat has finally reached the lighthouse. Augustus Carmichael walks beside her and agrees that they likely have landed. The novel ends as Lily turns to her painting, makes a final line through the middle and declares it complete. 'Yes, she thought, laying down her brush in extreme fatigue, I have had my vision.' ❀

# List of Characters in
## *To the Lighthouse*

**Mrs. Ramsay** is the first character the reader encounters. She spends most of the first part of the novel sitting at the window with her son James, reading him a story and reflecting on the intricacies of life. She has tremendous influence over the family and even after her death, her presence is significantly felt.

**Mr. Ramsay** is Mrs. Ramsay's husband. He is a philosopher who published an influential text when he was twenty-five but has not published anything as significant since. He is a volatile personality who remains cold and distant to almost everyone he encounters.

**Lily Briscoe** is a guest at the Ramsay's vacation home. She spends most of the novel painting a picture of the landscape. Mrs. Ramsay wants her to marry William Bankes, but she never does.

**William Bankes** is a bachelor who is also a guest at the Ramsay's guest home. He spends a great deal of time talking with Lily Briscoe.

**Charles Tansley** is an obsequious student of philosophy who holds Mr. Ramsay in high regard. The Ramsay children refer to him as 'The atheist.'

**Augustus Carmichael** is poet whose work is not fully recognized until after the war. He is a guest at the Ramsay's vacation home.

**James Ramsay** is one of the sons of Mr. and Mrs. Ramsay. In Part I of the novel, when he is still quite young, he gets terribly upset when his father insists that the weather will not allow him to travel to the lighthouse. Ten years later, when the novel resumes, James still harbors ill feelings toward his father.

**Cam Ramsay** is one of the daughters of Mr. and Mrs. Ramsay. In the final part of the novel, she travels to the lighthouse with her father and brother.

**Prue Ramsay** is one of the daughters of Mr. and Mrs. Ramsay. In the second Part of the novel, the reader is told that she died during childbirth.

**Andrew Ramsay** is one of the sons of Mr. and Mrs. Ramsay. In Part II, the reader is told that he was killed in battle.

**Nancy, Rose, Jasper, and Roger Ramsay** are all Ramsay children.

**Paul Rayley** is a family friend who gets engaged to Minta Doyle.

**Minta Doyle** is a family friend who gets engaged to Paul Rayley.

**Mrs. McNab** is the cleaning woman who looks after the Ramsay's vacation home. ❁

# Critical Views on
## *To the Lighthouse*

THOMAS A. VOGLER ON *TO THE LIGHTHOUSE*

[Thomas A. Vogler has been a professor of English Literature and Chairman of the Board of Studies in Literature at
the University of California at Santa Cruz. He has written
and edited several studies on English and American poets
and novelists, including a critical essay collection on
*Wuthering Heights*. In this excerpt, Vogler discusses the
novel's focus on childhood and parents.]

*To the Lighthouse* is unique among the novels for its focus directly on
childhood and parents, and in being located totally in a remote non-
urban setting. The two obviously go together, the invisible line
between Skye and the city reflecting that between childhood and
maturity. But even in Cornwall, the author's concern is still with the
kind of people she belonged to and knew well, the intellectual aris-
tocracy of the famous Bloomsbury Group. The Ramsays are *in* but
not *of* the inhabitants. Mrs. McNab is a representative of minimal
human consciousness, and Macalister and his son, though on the
boat, are not present. In her introduction to a book of biographies of
working class women, she wrote: "One could not be Mrs. Giles of
Durham, because one's body had never stood at the washtub; one's
hands had never wrung and scrubbed and chopped up whatever the
meat is that makes a miner's supper." Both the novel and this statement reflect the influence of the social dimensions of her life and
her method as a novelist. She worked from within, having done or
thought what she writes or having a firm ground for exercising intuition. To decry her failure to cover the full social spectrum in her
work, as has too often been done, is simply to wish she had been a
different person or to lack an awareness of who she was.

For a final but difficult point, it should be noticed that *To the
Lighthouse* reflects in its own way what Woolf meant by "all the usual
things I try to put in—life, death, etc." Mrs. Ramsay's drive for life,
for helping the poor, sending parcels, repairing the greenhouse, cov-
ering up the skull with her green shawl, arranging marriages, are
based on her intuitive knowledge of her "antagonist," death and

decay. At the back of her mind is always the knowledge of this antagonist she is fighting against, and an intuition that in death she might find the rest and calm and permanence in "eternity" which she longs for.

> . . . life being now strong enough to bear her on again, she began all this business, as a sailor not without weariness sees the wind fill his sail and yet hardly wants to be off again and thinks how, had the ship sunk, he would have whirled round and round and found rest on the floor of the sea.

Lily too has such moments in which she feels "her own headlong desire to throw herself off the cliff and be drowned looking for a pearl brooch on a beach." In all her work Virginia Woolf was asserting her life-affirming self against a comparable longing for rest, and the knowledge that it all came to death in the end, which might or might not be a new beginning. In Part II, when the screen door opens to let "Nothing" into the "house without a soul," Virginia Woolf is trying in her imagination to cross the line she stepped over when she walked into the Ouse, the line Septimus crossed when he leaped from the building in *Mrs. Dalloway*. As always, it is a glimpse beneath the waves on the surface, into the unknown depths which she knew she must some day penetrate to complete her life-long search for form:

> So loveliness reigned and stillness, and together made the shape of loveliness itself, a form from which life had parted; solitary like a pool at evening, far distant, seen from a train window, vanishing so quickly that the pool, pale in the evening, is scarcely robbed of its solitude, though once seen. Loveliness and stillness clasped hands in the bedroom, and among the shrouded jugs and sheeted chairs even the prying of the wind, and the soft nose of the clammy sea airs, rubbing, snuffling, and reiterating their questions—"Will you fade? Will you perish?"—scarcely disturbed the peace, the indifference, the air of pure integrity, as if the question they asked scarcely needed that they should answer: we remain.

> —Thomas A. Vogler, "Introduction," in *Twentieth Century Interpretations of* To the Lighthouse: *A Collection of Critical Essays,* Thomas A. Vogler, ed. (Englewood Cliffs, Prentice-Hall, Inc., 1970): pp. 14–15.

# Mitchell A. Leaska on Multiple Viewpoints in *To the Lighthouse*

[Mitchell A. Leaska has been a professor of English at New York University. He has published several essays and critical volumes, including *Virginia Woolf's Lighthouse: A Study in Critical Method*. In this excerpt, Leaska speaks on the play between narrative omniscience and character point of view.]

Occasionally Virginia Woolf presents, simultaneously, feelings shared, simultaneously, by two consciousnesses. In what follows, for example, James and his sister, Cam, are angrily preoccupied with their father's lack of consideration for them:

> Now they would sail on for hours like this, and Mr Ramsay would ask old Macalister a question—about the great storm last winter probably—and old Macalister would answer it, and they would puff their pipes together, and Macalister would take a tarry rope in his fingers, tying and untying some knot, and the boy would fish, and never say a word to anyone.

Once more, someone might argue that the Omniscient Narrator is reporting their thoughts and feelings. But again there are at least three clues which tend to contradict that assertion: in the first place, the sentence begins with 'Now', establishing the time as the fictional present which characterizes the contemporaneousness of interior monologue; secondly, the verb auxiliary, 'would', shifts all the verb forms to the subjunctive mood, thereby making all the actions they are thinking about actually contingent upon their father's whim; it indicates, moreover, that they are, possibly without realizing it, conjecturing—which the word, 'probably', would tend to support; third, the whole passage is one sentence consisting of six independent clauses joined by 'and'; and the resulting polysyndeton functions here to suggest the breathlessness of their adolescent impatience and anger. What is especially remarkable is that Mrs Woolf has convincingly created a mutually shared interior monologue with such seeming effortlessness. In fact, she uses 'they' twice in the passage, and intuitively the reader knows that the first 'they', referring to James and Cam, is the pronoun which establishes them as the *personae*. We might also observe, incidentally, how in the next sentence—keeping all the aforementioned elements constant, except for the possessive adjective, 'his', and the personal pronoun, 'he'—Mrs Woolf shifts us now into only James' mind and keeps us there briefly for two sentences, after which we are given more omniscient narration.

Another device the author utilizes to designate a particular narrator is the use of the 'tag' phrase, a phrase which eventually becomes associated with a narrator. When the reader becomes familiar with the narrators, the phrase begins to function as a signal for him, indicating that a shift has taken place as well as making it possible for him to identify the voice. Mrs Ramsay's favourite, 'after all', will illustrate the point (italics have been added to omniscient-narrator statements):

> And after all—after all (*here insensibly she drew herself together, physically, the sense of her own beauty becoming, as it did so seldom, present to her*)—after all, she had not generally any difficulty in making people like her; for instance, George Manning; Mr Wallace; famous as they were, they would come to her of an evening, quietly, and talk alone over her fire. *She bore about with her, she could not help knowing it, the torch of her beauty; she carried it erect into any room that she entered;* and after all, veil it as she might, and shrink from the monotony of bearing that it imposed on her, her beauty was apparent. She had been admired. She had been loved.

Around the first omniscient statement, Mrs Woolf has placed parentheses. Because she has not done so with the other two, they might easily pass unnoticed were it not for the fact that when we are back with Mrs Ramsay's thoughts, we realize that what she is thinking is essentially the same as the omniscient statements; only now the idea is repeated ostensibly in her idiom. And it is precisely here that the phrase, 'after all', takes on semantic significance: given to sympathy-seeking and self-depreciation, Mrs Ramsay recognizes—uses—her beauty as a *last resort,* only; *after all* else has failed to soothe and restore her sense of self, usually following some real or imagined injury—in this case, Carmichael's refusing her offer to get him anything from the village. 'After all', then, is an effective, appropriate, and telling introductory phrase for a woman who, under ordinary circumstances, feels she must 'veil' her beauty and 'shrink from the monotony of bearing that it imposed on her. . . .'

—Mitchell A. Leaska, *Virginia Woolf's Lighthouse: A Study in Critical Method* (New York, Columbia University Press, 1970): pp. 56–58.

# SUSAN RUBINOW GORSKY ON IMAGE AND SYMBOL

[Susan Rubinow Gorsky has been a professor of English at Cleveland State University. Her articles and essays have appeared in such journals as *Modern Fiction Studies, Modern Drama,* and *The Journal of Popular Culture*. In this excerpt, Gorsky speaks on the relationship between symbol and structure in the novel.]

*To the Lighthouse* is like a two-act play with an entr'acte, each "act" (or section) dominated by the symbol which is its title. "The Window," the first and longest section, is set early one September afternoon and evening at the summer home of the Ramsay family in the Hebrides, off the Scottish coast. The cast includes Mr. and Mrs. Ramsay, their eight children, a half dozen friends, and a few others— a cook, a maid, some villagers. Through the first half of this section a drawing-room window provides a two-way frame. Inside the house Mrs. Ramsay reads to James, her youngest son, or helps him find pictures to cut out, while her mind roams through memories and considers problems of interest to her or her family. Occasionally her attention is drawn outside, and she looks through the window at her husband pacing the porch or at Lily Briscoe painting on the lawn. Her husband often looks at her or stops to talk, and Lily, an artist in her early thirties, regards the picture of mother and son framed by the window as part of the composition of her painting. The effect is partly ironic, because for all her beauty Mrs. Ramsay is not simply frozen as an object of art, and for all her veneration Lily plans to incorporate Mrs. Ramsay into the painting only as a triangular shadow. Other characters are introduced as they are remembered by or come into contact with one of these three: William Bankes, the scientist who fusses about properly cooked vegetables; Charles Tansley, a young scholar whose praise comforts Mr. Ramsay but whose insecure aggressiveness annoys the rest of the family; Augustus Carmichael, a poet of no reputation whose beard is stained by opium; Paul Rayley and Minta Doyle, who fulfill Mrs. Ramsay's unspoken but obvious wishes by becoming engaged; and the children, from the beautiful Prue, and the mathematically gifted Andrew to James and Cam, at six and seven still too young to join the family at dinner. Nothing out of the ordinary happens on this particular day. Mr. Ramsay angers James by interrupting and by predicting that bad weather will preclude a trip to the Lighthouse next day; Lily works at her painting; Nancy and Andrew are startled on a walk with Paul and Minta by seeing the newly engaged pair embrace; Mrs. Ramsay presides over dinner for the large gathering, helps to allay her husband's fears that his fame as a writer of philosophy will not last, but cannot tell him that she loves him.

As "Time Passes" (the entr'acte) begins, the lights are extinguished and the cast of characters prepare for sleep. As it ends, some of the same people repeat this action: Mr. Carmichael stays up latest, reading Virgil. When the curtain rises on "The Lighthouse," the last "act," Lily is at breakfast planning to complete her painting, and James, Cam, and Mr. Ramsay are preparing to sail to the Lighthouse. However, it is ten years later. A decade has passed in the brief, lyrical interlude which occupies less than one-tenth of the novel, just about thirty pages. One night can blur into ten years because without human intervention or measurement, the division of a day into hours or a year into months has no purpose. During the years of the Ramsay's absence "time" merely "passes," as the title asserts. But in this period Mrs. Ramsay dies, Prue marries and dies in childbirth, Andrew is killed in the First World War, and Mr. Carmichael achieves the fame which Mr. Ramsay so desires. In an ordinary novel, such events would be emphasized but here they are deliberately underplayed, presented in stark factual reports, bracketed off from the poetic description of the uninterrupted passage of days and seasons. The physical intervention of two women who prepare the house for the Ramsays' return can rescue the house from "the sands of oblivion," "the pool of Time" into which it was sinking. The house is rescued and most of the people return, some to complete projects begun in the first act. "The Lighthouse" section is dominated by Mr. Ramsays' determined pilgrimage to that symbol of the past, as James and Cam are dominated by their father and forced against their wills to participate in his ritual of remembrance. In scenes which alternate with those of the trip, Lily also pays homage to her memory of Mrs. Ramsay, finally completing the painting which depends upon her vision of the older woman. James and Cam's hatred of their father gives way to love as their boat nears the Lighthouse. "He has landed." Lily says as she stands by her easel looking toward the Lighthouse she can barely see in the distance; "It is finished," she adds, in reference to both the symbolic journey and her painting.

—Susan Rubinow Gorsky, *Virginia Woolf* (Boston, Twayne Publishers, 1978): pp. 99–100.

## Louise A. DeSalvo on 1897: Virginia Woolf at Fifteen

[Louise A. DeSalvo has been a professor at Hunter College, City University of New York. She is the author of *Virginia Woolf's First Voyage*. In this excerpt, DeSalvo speaks on Woolf's inspiration for the novel.]

In 1924 Virginia Woolf published an essay entitled "*The Antiquary*" in the *New Republic*. It is likely that she began the essay on or about 16 October 1924. On 17 October Woolf wrote the diary entry recording her inspiration for *To the Lighthouse*—"I see already the Old Man." Beginning her review of *The Antiquary* probably brought up memories and unresolved issues from 1897—the year Leslie Stephen read the work aloud to his children—most particularly, from 27 January, when Woolf records, "Father began the Antiquary to us" through Wednesday, 31 March, when she records that either he or she completed the novel. This is the period when Woolf's freedom was curtailed, when she accompanied Stella and Jack to Bognor against her will. So much of *To the Lighthouse* explores the emotional confluence of the events of 1897—the life-giving yet stifling and inhibiting presence of a mother figure, then her sudden death and absence; the lovable yet irritatingly infantile, dependent father figure; the need to come to terms with these two as parents and with the absence of the mother and continuing presence of the father while simultaneously trying to construct an identity derived from each and yet separate from both. All these reflect Woolf's situation in 1897. And it is fascinating to note that one of the prototypes of the characters of the Antiquary, according to Lockhart's life of Scott, which Woolf read during this year, was John *Ramsay* of Ochtertyre.

Woolf referred to *The Antiquary* in "The Window" section of *To the Lighthouse*. Mrs. Ramsay comes into a room where Mr. Ramsay is "reading something that moved him very much. He was half smiling and then she knew he was controlling his emotion. He was tossing the pages over. He was acting it—perhaps he was thinking himself the person in the book. She wondered what book it was. Oh, it was one of old Sir Walter's she saw."

Later Mr. Ramsay is described as reading about "poor Steenie's drowning and Mucklebackit's sorrow." Thoughts of his wife, his family, and himself become intermingled with his response to the Scott novel:

> This man's strength and sanity, his feeling for straightforward simple things, these fishermen, the poor old crazed creature in Mucklebackit's cottage made him feel so vigorous, so relieved of something that he felt roused and triumphant and could not choke back his tears. Raising the book a little to hide his face, he let them fall and shook his head from side to side and forgot himself completely . . . forgot his own bothers and failures completely in poor Steenie's drowning and Mucklebackit's sorrow (that was Scott at his best) and the astonishing delight and feeling of vigour that it gave him.

This portrait of Mr. Ramsay, a fictional surrogate for Leslie Stephen, was no doubt based upon Woolf's memory of her father's reading *The Antiquary* to the family in 1897. In the Scott novel the scene Mr. Ramsay reads is as follows:

> The body was laid in its coffin within the wooden bedstead which the young fisher had occupied while alive. At a little distance stood the father, whose rugged, weatherbeaten countenance, shaded by his grizzled hair, had faced many a stormy night and night-like day. He was apparently revolving his loss in his mind with that strong feeling of painful grief peculiar to harsh and rough characters, which almost breaks forth into hatred against the world and all that remain in it after the beloved object is withdrawn. The old man had made the most desperate efforts to save his son, and had only been withheld by main force from renewing them at a moment when, without the possibility of assisting the sufferer, he himself must have perished.

> —Louise A. DeSalvo, "1897: Virginia Woolf at Fifteen" in *Virginia Woolf: A Feminist Slant,* Jane Marcus, ed. (Lincoln, University of Nebraska Press, 1983): pp. 93–94.

# Susan Dick on The Tunneling Process: Some Aspects of Virginia Woolf's Use of Memory and the Past

[Susan Dick has taught at Queen's University, Kingston Ontario. She has been the editor of George Moore's *Confessions* and of the holograph *To the Lighthouse*. In this excerpt, Dick explains how Woolf expanded and refined the role of memory which was prominent in earlier novels such as *Mrs. Dalloway*.]

Young people abound in *To the Lighthouse*. Here Woolf expands and refines the narrative method of *Mrs. Dalloway* and her use of memory, like so much else, is far more subtle and varied here than in her earlier narratives. The ways that the characters remember the past, the things they remember, and in Part III the relation between the process of remembering and the creation of a work of art, are all aspects of *To the Lighthouse* that I wish briefly to explore.

The central characters in *Mrs. Dalloway* draw their memories from a common pool of memories. Woolf will use this device again in *The Waves* where her six speakers share a common childhood. In *To the Lighthouse*, however, she does not link characters in this way. Nor does she dramatize her central character, Mrs. Ramsay, by using her personal memories as the background against which her present life is placed. The silent question Mrs. Ramsay asks herself as she sits down to dinner, 'But what have I done with my life?' does not initiate a train of memories as it would have done in Mrs. Dalloway's mind. Mrs. Ramsay's past is drawn in sketchily and the events which have made her what she is are not disclosed. 'What was there behind it—her beauty and splendour?' the narrator wonders, echoing the curiosity of others. 'Had he blown his brains out, they asked, had he died the week before they were married—some other, earlier lover, of whom rumours reached one?' Mrs. Ramsay's thought that 'she had had experiences which need not happen to every one (she did not name them to herself)' is as close as she comes to recalling the specific events which might be grounds for these rumours. When she thinks of her marriage, her thoughts centre around general memories of things her husband has done or said and on general regrets or concerns, and she recalls only two specific scenes from her early life. The first of these is prompted during dinner by Mr.

Bankes's reference to her old friends the Mannings. 'Oh, she could remember it as if it were yesterday—going on the river, feeling very cold.' This recollection becomes for her that 'dream land, that unreal but fascinating place, the Mannings' drawing room at Marlow twenty years ago; where one moved about without haste or anxiety, for there was no future to worry about.' She sees this memory as she will later see the successful dinner party, as something 'immune from change'. Mrs. Ramsay links memory and the escape from mutability in a way that recalls Clarissa's thoughts about immortality and foreshadows Lily's about art.

The other scene Mrs. Ramsay recalls from the past gives us a glimpse of Mr. Ramsay as he was when 'she had first known him, gaunt but gallant; helping her out of a boat, she remembered; with delightful ways'. Perhaps she has told Lily of this scene or perhaps it is coincidence that leads Lily to imagine one like it ten years later as she attempts to recapture the past and complete her painting.

> —Susan Dick, "The Tunnelling Process: Some Aspects of Virginia Woolf's Use of Memory and the Past" in *Virginia Woolf: New Critical Essays*, Patricia Clements and Isobel Grundy, eds. (London, Vision Press, 1983): pp. 189–190.

〰

### ALICE VAN BUREN KELLEY ON *TO THE LIGHTHOUSE*: BLOOMSBURY ART THEORY AND WOOLF'S CONCEPT OF ART

[Alice van Buren Kelley has been a professor of English at the University of Pennsylvania. She is the author of *The Novels of Virginia Woolf: Fact and Vision* and To the Lighthouse: *The Marriage of Life and Art*. In this excerpt, van Buren Kelley discusses the influence of Post-Impressionist art on the novel.]

When Lily Briscoe sets up her easel on the Ramsay's lawn and faces a blank canvas onto which she must transfer her vision of what is before her, arranged to express an elusive answer to "a simple question," "What is the meaning of life?" she makes explicit an issue that is implicit in most of the novel. For *To the Lighthouse* is among other things a novel about art, what it aims for, what it might achieve, and what means it should employ to reach its end. These questions about art are presumably hovering in the lives of all serious writers; but for Virginia Woolf art theory was as much in the air as cigarette smoke during the many evenings when she would sit talking with her sister and her friends. Vanessa was a painter, married to Clive Bell, whose cocky little book on art had caused much talk in its day. When Clive moved to the outskirts of her life, Roger Fry, for a time, moved to the center, becoming so important a part of Virginia's life as well that it was she who was asked to write his biography after he died. In his day, Roger Fry was one of his country's most influential art critics. His organizing of the First Post-Impressionist Exhibition in November 1910 shook accepted notions of art and his lectures converted many to his views. Virginia Woolf, too, found that his ideas soon captured her imagination.

"Why is it," she asks in her biography of Fry, "that Roger Fry's criticism has for the common seer something of the enthrallment of a novel, something of the excitement of a detective story while it is strictly about the art of painting and nothing else?" The easiest answer to her question is to offer another quotation, one from Fry's *Vision and Design*, published just five years before Woolf began *To the Lighthouse*. Woolf chose this passage as one to cite in her biography, perhaps because it centers on a particular concept of reality that surfaces in her own writing like a leitmotif. In it, Fry is attempting to explain to his audience the aims of Cézanne and the other postimpressionists:

> Now, these artists do not seek to give what can, after all, be but a pale reflex of actual appearances, but to arouse the conviction of a new and definite reality. They do not seek to imitate form, but to create form; not to imitate life, but to find an equivalent for life. By that I mean that they wish to make images which by the clearness of their logical structure, and by their closely-knit unity of texture, shall appeal to our disinterested and contemplative imagination with something of the same vividness as the things of actual life appeal to our practical activities. In fact, they aim not at illusion but at reality.

> —Alice van Buren Kelley, To the Lighthouse: *The Marriage of Life and Art* (Boston, Twayne Publishers, 1987): pp. 61–62.

# Plot Summary of
## *Orlando*

*Orlando,* one of Virginia Woolf's most ambitious and comic novels, takes the form of a fantastical biography in which the hero/heroine, Orlando, lives through three different centuries and metamorphoses from a male into female. **The novel opens** in the Sixteenth Century as Orlando, now a boy of sixteen, is in the attic of his house, slicing his sword through he air, and pretend-fighting with a skull hanging by a cord from the rafters. As Orlando exercises his imagination, the biographer of this tale, who is expressing delight in capturing such a provocative figure, addresses the reader.

When Orlando tires of play fighting, he sits down at a table and starts writing poetry. The reader is told of his smooth yet abstract style, where 'Vice, Crime, Misery were the personages of his drama.' Eventually he lays down his pen and walks out of his house and into the woods. He stops beside an oak tree and gazes at the landscape until he hears the blaring of a trumpet, announcing the arrival of Queen Elizabeth. He races off to greet her with the rest of the towns-people. That night, the queen, a distant relative of Orlando's, enters into his house and kisses him while he is asleep. Soon after, he is beckoned to her side where he becomes her lover until she sees him kissing another woman. Afterward, Orlando spends a period of time in blue-collar society, where he takes on another lover, eventually growing tired of the lifestyle and returning to his privileged surroundings.

Following Orlando's return to upper class living, he spends significant time with three young ladies (Clorinda, Favilla, and Euphrosyne, as he refers to them in his poetry). These relationships are successive, the last one ending at the beginning of the Great Frost.

The reader is given a playful, fantastic account of the Great Frost, where 'birds froze in mid-air,' and there was a wide 'solidification of unfortunate wayfarers who had been turned literally to stone where they stood.' King James turns the frozen areas into social carnivals and fosters a vibrant social environment. Orlando meets the Russian Princess Marousha Stanilovska Dagmar Natasha Iliana Romanovitch, who speaks French and is known as the Muscovite by the townspeople and Sasha by Orlando. He falls in love with her, despite being betrothed to Euphrosyne, who the reader learns is really named Lady Margaret O'Brien O'Dare O'Reilly Tyrconnel. Orlando undergoes drastic shifts in mood, from melancholy to elation. Though there is a scheduled date for Orlando's wedding to Lady Margaret, he is so consumed by his love for Sasha that he feels little shame in breaking the engagement, planning instead to return to Russia with Sasha.

Orlando and his beloved walk to a Russian ship where Sasha boards to get some of her clothing. Orlando waits for over an hour before his insecurities get the best of him. He witnesses a sailor helping Sasha with her bags, and throws a temper tantrum. Though Sasha is upset at his childishness, she makes up with him. Still emotionally jarred, Orlando makes arrangements for them to meet the following night. But when the next night arrives, Orlando waits through a rainstorm for Sasha, before it is clear that she will not show. Chapter One ends as Orlando flees to the Thames River which is raging with icy flood waters, barreling icebergs over groups of people. He rides his horse to the sea where the 'ships of the Ambassadors had seemed immovably frozen.' He finds the Muscovite ship, leaps from his horse into the water and shouts obscenities about Sasha.

**Chapter Two** opens with the biographer's set up of Orlando's first trance. Disgraced by prominent society, he moves out to the country where he falls asleep and does not wake for seven days. When he finally opens his eyes, he banishes everyone from his room and begins to live a life of predominant solitude. He laments the loss of his first real love and falls into periodic states of extreme melancholy. To help ease the burden of reality, he starts to read incessantly, eventually leading him to take up the pen himself. It is here that the biographer reveals that Orlando has fallen into similar states before, having already written, 'before he was turned twenty-five, some forty-seven plays, histories, romances, poems; some in prose, some in verse; some in French, some in Italian; all romantic, and all long.' After undergoing the rigors and emotional volatility of writing, in which he 'could not decide whether he was the divinest genius or the greatest fool in the world,' he makes the decision to reenter society, concluding that he is meant to be a writer and that social interaction is necessary for writing as well as internal stability.

Orlando decides to send an admiring note to the poet and critic Nicholas Greene, requesting that he accept transportation to his estate to eat and discuss the art of writing. The poet accepts the offer and takes advantage of an extended stay with Orlando. When he finally decides to leave, Orlando, who is both relieved and saddened, gives him one of his own plays and asks him to look it over.

When Greene returns home, he writes a biting satire of his experience; 'no one could doubt that the young Lord who was roasted was Orlando.' After reading Greene's piece entitled 'Visit to a Nobleman in the Country', Orlando burnt every poem he had ever written except for one, 'The Oak Tree', and vowed that he had had enough of mankind. It is here that the biographer tells of his vast solitude and the passing of time where over a hundred years have elapsed, though Orlando has aged only to thirty. Still hurt by Nicholas Greene's satire, he makes a vow that from then on he will write only for himself.

Orlando undergoes a transformation. It starts with the redecoration of his estate and leads to his new drive to throw extravagant parties and play an active role in society. He wins back the favor of the public, particularly women and poets for whom he is particularly gracious. He writes only in private, working exclusively on his poem 'The Oak Tree'. One day, Orlando encounters the eccentric 'Archduchess Harriet Griselda of Finster-Aarhorn and Scandop-Boom in the Roumanian territory,' who had ridden her horse through Orlando's property, claiming that she was hoping to meet him. She takes up residence in town and spends a concentrated period of time with Orlando. When the courtship becomes too much, he asks King George to send him to Constantinople as an Ambassador. It is here that Chapter Two comes to an end.

**Chapter Three** opens with the biographer explaining that despite Orlando's increased social and political role (in Constantinople), there is an unfortunate lack of information about this particular portion of his life. The revolution that erupted during this time and the subsequent fire that followed had apparently wiped away most traces of activity.

Orlando is said to have sought out few companions, choosing instead to devote himself to his work, his rank eventually elevated to Duke. Orlando uses the opportunity of his new rank to arrange an enormous festival, which the narrative presents in the form of various incomplete journal accounts. Following the festivity, Orlando goes back to his room to sleep. When he does not wake up at the usual time, a doctor is summoned. While the doctor is trying to arouse him, Orlando's secretaries search through the documents that surround his bed and find a marriage contract indicating that sometime during the night he married a gypsy dancer, Rosina Lolita. While Orlando sleeps, three women, meant to symbolize the Lady of Purity, Lady of Chastity, and the Lady of Modesty, enter his room and recite cryptic messages while dancing around the sleeping Duke. This ceremony seems to evoke the end of Orlando's second trance, from which he awakens as a woman. The biographer does not attempt to make any scientific explanation about Orlando's transformation, but states simply 'Orlando was a man till the age of thirty; when he became a woman and has remained so ever since.'

Orlando goes off to live in a gypsy village where they make her feel shame in the excessive wealth of her family. She eventually concludes that she must leave the village and return to England. Chapter Three ends as Orlando, now a woman, boards a merchant ship traveling to England.

**Chapter Four** opens on the ship where Orlando first reflects on her new gender, realizing 'with a start the penalties and the privileges of her position.' Throughout the journey, she is treated graciously by the distinguished Captain Nicholas Benedict Bartolus. When the ship begins its final approach, the captain points out the various sights in London. Orlando had not seen London since the Great Frost and was overcome with emotion. She weeps openly, feeling that it is more acceptable to do so as a female.

Orlando returns to her estate where she is greeted by the familiar faces of her servants. She reacquaints herself with her surroundings, and is particularly happy to be back. She finds new inspiration here and continues work on her poem 'The Oak Tree'. It is not long after her return that the Archduchess Harriet arrives to see her. The Archduchess reveals that she is really a man, Archduke Harry, and had dressed as a woman when they had met earlier in hopes of winning Orlando's favor. Archduke Harry comes back every day after that in an effort to continue his courtship. Orlando grows bored by the Archduke's company. She decides to cheat at a silly game in hopes of turning him off. The Archduke eventually acknowledges Orlando's deception and declares that a person capable of such an act was not worth marrying. Orlando is relieved, deciding that now she should really look for a lover.

Orlando spends time in London, interacting with prominent literary figures, including Addison, Pope and Swift, all of whom she invites back to her home for tea and conversation. Orlando soon tires of the company of these wits. Chapter Four ends as a dark cloud hovers over England and the clock strikes midnight. 'The Eighteenth century was over; the Nineteenth century had begun.'

**Chapter Five** begins with discussion of the black cloud which appeared over England and never went away, forcing everyone to adjust to the ubiquitous dampness. It is apparently this dampness that is responsible for the habit of hot drinks and for the ivy that surrounds many buildings in England.

Orlando decides that the time has come for her to finish her poem 'The Oak Tree,' which she has been working on since 1586, when she was still a young boy. She also decides that the time has come for her to find a husband. She goes for a walk in the fields, and on a whim, starts to run, tripping and breaking her ankle. A man named Marmaduke Bonthrop Shelmerdine, Esquire, finds her. 'A few minutes later, they became engaged.'

Orlando and Shelmerdine spend the ensuing days in conversation, getting to know the more superficial points about each other. It is during this time that a letter arrives for Orlando regarding her estate, which had been in dispute ever since she returned home from Constantinople as a woman. The results are all favorable, though the legal bills have left her monetarily poor. Chapter Five ends with the marriage of Orlando and Shelmerdine.

The final chapter, **Chapter Six**, opens with Orlando reflecting on her marriage and whether it makes a difference if her husband has to travel most of his days as she hopes to write poetry with much of her time. She turns her reflection to the page and starts adding lines to 'The Oak Tree'. She writes incessantly for over a year until finally she declares she is done.

Orlando realizes that as she was writing, the world was going on without her. She feels a sudden need to interact with humans. She barely hesitates before heading to London. When she gets there she realizes that she had carried 'The Oak Tree' inside the bosom of her dress, as was her habit. Soon after discovering her manuscript, she sees Nicholas Greene, the poet and critic who had written the scandalous satire centuries ago. Greene invites her to lunch where he speaks ill of the young writers of the day. Just as Orlando concludes that Greene is as vile as he has always been, a clasp in her blouse opens and her manuscript, 'The Oak Tree', falls onto the table.

Greene grabs the manuscript and starts to read it. He praises its honesty and insists that it must be published immediately. Greene takes 'The Oak Tree' and they part ways. Orlando walks the streets and notices all the changes that have occurred since her last visit. She reflects on the unusual nature of Life, thinking of her chance encounter with Greene. She decides to telegraph her husband, telling him in their secret dialect what has taken place and how she is feeling. She goes into a bookshop and asks for everything of importance to be sent to her home.

She walks across the street to Hyde Park and starts to read a journal of literary criticism. The criticism reminds her of the satire that Greene had written and she becomes upset. As tears well in her eyes, she spots a toy boat and imagines it is a life size boat crossing the Atlantic. She becomes elated again. Following this fluctuation of emotions, she leaves the park.

At this point, the biographer jumps into abstract narrative that leads obscurely to the birth of Orlando's son, an event that the biographer acknowledges will take some readers by surprise. 'But let the reader take courage; nothing of the same sort is going to happen today, which is not, by any means, the same day.' Orlando revels at the enormous changes that seem to be in effect. Suddenly she is struck by the blaring of a clock. 'Ten times she was struck. In fact it was ten o'clock in the morning. It was the eleventh of October. It was 1928. It was the present moment.'

Shocked by the changing face of time, Orlando rushes out of her house, jumps into her car and drives into traffic as if she had been doing it her entire life. She stops at a department store and takes the elevator upstairs, consulting her shopping list as she ascends. While in the process of buying bed sheets, she sees a heavy Russian woman whom she believes to be Sasha. She becomes upset and leaves the store.

While Orlando drives, she reflects on her many selves, wondering what it means to be a thirty-six-year-old woman now driving a motorcar. Everything she passes—trees, people, crops—she relates to in some nostalgic way. It is here that the reader is told of the prizes and overall acclaim that accompanied the printing of 'The Oak Tree'. The biographer acknowledges the unusual manner in which the events of Orlando's life have been revealed, but notes that 'when we write of a woman, everything is out of place—culminations and per-oration; the accent never falls where it does with a man.'

When Orlando makes it home, she walks through her estate and into the woods where she climbs the same hill she had climbed in the beginning of the novel, stopping by the same oak tree. She takes a signed copy of her manuscript out of the bosom of her dress and buries it. While standing beside this great oak, she reflects on her success and the superficiality of material goods. The novel ends with her crying out for Shelmerdine, just before the twelfth stroke of midnight, in the time of the present. ❀

# List of Characters in
## *Orlando*

**Orlando** is the hero/heroine of the novel and the first character the reader encounters. Orlando lives through three hundred years and transforms from male to female. Orlando spends a portion of each century working on the poem 'The Oak Tree' which eventually gets published to wide acclaim. Though Orlando experiences love initially as a boy, it is the female Orlando who eventually marries.

**Sasha** is Orlando's first love. She is a Russian princess who stands Orlando up and breaks his heart.

**Rosina Lolita** is a gypsy dancer whom Orlando marries before he transforms into a woman.

**Nicholas Greene** is a famous poet and critic. He writes a slanderous satire of his visit to the male Orlando's home. When he meets Orlando again (hundreds of years later when Orlando is a mature woman), he reads her manuscript and eventually gets it published.

**Marmaduke Bonthrop Shelmardine** finds the mature female Orlando after she breaks her ankle. They fall in love and get married.

**Lady Margaret** is engaged to Orlando early in the novel, but he leaves her to pursue Sasha.

**Archduchess/Archduke Harriet/Harry Griselda** tries to court Orlando, first by dressing up as a female, and then again after he reveals he is a male.

**Captain Nicholas Benedict Bartolus** is the captain of the English ship that Orlando takes from Constantinople to England, just after becoming a woman. ❀

# Critical Views on
## *Orlando*

JEAN GUIGUET ON THE SELF, LIFE AND ARTISTIC
CREATION

[Jean Guiguet has been a prominent French scholar and
critic for several decades. Guiguet's study of Virginia Woolf,
*Virginia Woolf and Her Works,* was one of the first comprehensive volumes on the body of Woolf's work. In this
excerpt, Jean Guiguet speaks on Woolf's treatment of love.]

Her marriage to Leonard Woolf in 1912 seems not noticeably to
have modified her way of life nor the course of her inner develop-
ment. Love, although it takes a leading place in her two first novels,
appears there less as a total upheaval, a profound revision of values,
than as a particular experience in the field of human relations, an
important one no doubt but essentially of the same nature as other
personal contacts. It would be easy to conclude from this that the
real nature of passion was alien to Virginia Woolf. The absence of
any evidence to the contrary tempts one to accept this interpretation. However, the word passion should here be taken in a strictly
limited sense: the storm of the senses, the absorption of one's whole
being by the sexual instinct are things absent from Virginia Woolf's
world; perhaps, indeed, she was unfamiliar with them. This hypoth-
esis, though plausible, is far from certain. Her work itself is an
ambiguous document, from which one might extract contrary evidence: the exclusion of sexuality from her art might just as well
imply that it played so healthy and normal a part in her life as to
require no sublimation.

Her first reaction to Joyce's *Ulysses* may give some weight to this
interpretation, particularly if we note the comment with which she
justifies her disappointment and disgust. "But I think if you are
anaemic, as Tom [T. S. Eliot] is, there is a glory in blood. Being fairly
normal myself I am soon ready for the classics again." None the less,
there are certain reservations to be made about this leaning towards
"classicism", this normality of temperament. Art is not solely nour-
ished on repressed, perverted or sublimated instincts; it is not only
an indirect, but also a direct expression. A certain sensual warmth is

surely permissible, short of finding "glory in blood"; but this, too, is admittedly repugnant to Virginia Woolf. Certain aspects of physical life seem too violent for her over-sensitive nature. Thus she confesses: "I don't like the physicalness of having children of one's own. This occurred to me at Rodmell; but I never wrote it down. I can dramatise myself a parent, it is true. And perhaps I have killed the feeling instinctively; or perhaps nature does."

Is this shrinking from motherhood part of that rejection of mere femininity, of passivity, of purely organic and instinctive creation, against which the virile traits of her nature asserted themselves, or is it one aspect of a more general denial of any physical relationship between human beings? I have already pointed out how little place the physical element takes in her pictures of love. The only book in which it may be glimpsed—smuggled in, as it were, behind a screen of satire and fantasy—is *Orlando*. And it was precisely during the writing of *Orlando* that she made the comment just quoted, on December 20, 1927. In the following paragraph, on the same day, we read: "I am still writing the third chapter of *Orlando*"—that third chapter in which truth breaks out to the sound of trumpets, where truth springs naked from its sleep in the shape of Orlando transformed into a woman. True, the subject here is Vita—V. Sackville-West—whose "form combined in one the strength of a man and a woman's grace." But who can boast of being able to discern unhesitatingly in a portrait what belongs to the model and what is the painter's? Added to which, if these thoughts lay in the background of Orlando, they remained unembodied in words until she watched her sister's children in a play: "The little creatures acting moved my infinitely sentimental throat." This emotion lends pathos to the lines in which Virginia Woolf assesses the two possible ways taken by her sister and herself: to be a mother or to be a writer.

—Jean Guiguet, *Virginia Woolf and Her Works* (New York, Harcourt, Brace & World, Inc., 1962): pp. 66–68.

## Avrom Fleishman on *Orlando* and 'The world created by that vision'

[Avrom Fleishman has been a professor of English at The Johns Hopkins University. He has published several books including *Conrad's Politics, The English Historical Novel,* and *A Reading of Mansfield Park.* In this excerpt, Fleishman speaks on the fusion of fiction and biography.]

*Orlando* is not merely an infusion of "the literary element" into the biographical form but a genuine fusion of fiction and biography, with all the attendant contradictions that a mixture of history and art entails. One of the ways in which literature and biography are mixed here is in the incorporation of literary texts, from passing allusions to lengthy quotations, into the fabric of the work. A number of scholars have shown that some of the verses which Orlando composes are based on the writings of the Sackville family, from the Renaissance Thomas Sackville's Induction to *The Mirror for Magistrates* (quoted in the manuscript but replaced by intentionally trivial lines in the published text) to passages from Vita Sackville-West's set of georgics, *The Land,* which is the original of Orlando's poem, "The Oak Tree." The inclusion of portions of the biographical subject's writings is by no means unusual in the genre, but is here raised to a principle: ". . . biographers and critics might save themselves all their labours if readers would only take this advice. For when we read: [five lines of *The Rape of the Lock* quoted]—we know as if we heard him how Mr. Pope's tongue flickered like a lizard's, how his eyes flashed, how his hand trembled, how he loved, how he lied, how he suffered. In short, every secret of a writer's soul, every experience of his life, every quality of his mind is written large in his works. . . ." We have here an extension of the style-is-the-man dictum to biography, for if style fully revealed a man's traits and even inner experience it would be enough to incorporate samples of his work to evoke his authentic nature.

Woolf does not, of course, believe that any such simple equivalence of effect is likely, and the above quotation goes on to acknowledge, perhaps facetiously, the continued need for critics and biographers who will relate the text to the writer: ". . . yet we require critics to explain the one and biographers to expound the other. That time hangs heavy on people's hands is the only explanation of the monstrous growth." Despite her limited expectations of success-fully evoking the presence of the man by citing his work, Woolf does go on to quote entire paragraphs of Addison and of Swift, in each case claiming to "hold that gentleman, cocked hat and all, in the hollow of our hands." Elsewhere, *Orlando* attempts to revivify the life and times of its biographical subject by directly or indirectly quoting his contemporaries. Not only is Shakespeare observed in the act of composition, but Orlando is described as seeing a street per-formance of *Othello,* which brings three lines of the post-murder speech into the fabric of the text (from act 5, scene 2, 11. 99–101). Sir Thomas Browne's prose is not directly quoted but its effects are richly described: "Like an incantation rising from all parts of the room, from the night wind and the moonlight, rolled the divine melody of those words which, lest they should outstare this page, we will leave where they lie entombed, not dead, embalmed rather, so fresh is their colour, so sound their breathing. . . ."

—Avrom Fleishman, *Virginia Woolf: A Critical Reading* (Baltimore, The Johns Hopkins University Press, 1975): pp. 137–138.

## T. E. Apter on *Orlando* and the Problem of Being a Woman

[T. E. Apter, born in Chicago, moved to Britain where she studied music and philosophy. Her previous publications include two novels, *Silken Lines and Silver Hooks* and *Adonis' Garden,* and a book of literary criticism, *Thomas Mann: The Devil's Advocate.* In this excerpt, Apter speaks on the physical and psychological changes that occur in the novel.]

Orlando undergoes one dramatic physical change from man to woman, and then undergoes more gradual psychological changes. First she discovers the pleasure of resisting, and then yielding to, men's advances. She becomes vain and timid and frightened of ghosts. She discovers the joy of having a protector, and this joy com-pensates her for the discomfort of her constricting skirts. Orlando realises that she must now suffer the culture her former male self endorsed: to be a woman means that she will never again be able to swear or to display violence or to sentence a man to death; nor will she be able to prance down Whitehall on a war-horse or lead an army or wear medals. Despite her regrets, she discovers that she is beginning to despise the sex to which she once belonged:

> 'To fall from a masthead,' she thought, 'because you see a woman's ankles; to dress up like a Guy Fawkes and parade the streets, so that women may praise you; to deny a woman teaching lest she may laugh at you; to be the slave of the frailest chit in petticoats, and yet to go about as if you were the Lords of creation. —Heavens!' she thought, 'what fools they make of us—what fools we are!'

What is worst in a man, then, is seen in his relation to woman. Clichés are self-propagating, and one sex frequently tries, for the sake of the other sex, to fulfil its stereotype. Thus the eighteenth-century prostitute abandons her frail, clinging manner when she discovers that Orlando is a woman; it is with relief she steps out of her ridiculous role and converses honestly with her companion, as she could not do with a man.

The difficulty is that in criticizing stereotypes, Virginia Woolf does not escape them, but merely notes them with an expert eye. At their best the clichés are burlesqued, as when Orlando's conversation with Archduke Harry turns to love because they have exhausted the subject of the weather, and because men and women can converse only on these two subjects. In her anger the author sometimes twists clichés (as long as women are writing 'little notes' it is permissible for them to write; as long as they are thinking about men, it is permissible for them to think) but the result is neither startling nor remarkable. For the most part Woolf's criticism of society is a slipshod mockery and analysis of customs. She makes much of the nineteenth-century crinoline that was an attempt to disguise woman's perpetual pregnancy, and of the wedding ring that, the author claims, poisons the being. Her descriptions of the seventeenth-century coteries, however, read like a fine crib of Proust's account of various social circles: different hostesses create different illusions in their drawing-rooms—one creates an atmosphere of profundity, another of happiness, another of wit; but when Pope arrives and says three witty things all in the space of a few minutes, the atmosphere is destroyed. The poet is not a creator but a destroyer of illusions; that is his importance and power.

—T. E. Apter, *Virginia Woolf: A Study of Her Novels* (New York, New York University Press, 1979): pp. 104–5.

⊕

## JUDY LITTLE ON THE POLITICS OF HOLIDAY: WOOLF'S LATER NOVELS

[Judy Little has been a professor of English at Southern Illinois University, Carbondale. She is the author of *Keats as a Narrative Poet: A Test of Invention*. In this excerpt, Little relates the psychological changes with the historical changes.]

Orlando's psychological relation to the historical periods through which she passes is hard to define exactly. She and any given historical milieu seem to reflect each other, and yet most readers agree with Orlando (and with Orlando's servants, who enthusiastically recognize and admire either him or her) that the main character does not change in any essential way; only Orlando's social behavior varies from age to age. The major joke of the sex change is that it makes little real difference in Orlando's character; by implication, most expressions of sex differences are cultural and not biological. The more Orlando changes, the more she stays the same. And yet the changes that she witnesses, and usually participates in, are major ones, not merely evolutions of manner but revolutions of basic norms and codes, those which, in the real, non-fictional world, are rooted in primary socialization; certainly the behavior of the sexes is so rooted. Orlando herself realizes this as she tries, on the ship, to adjust to the fact that sailors may drop off the rigging with excitement if she fails to keep her ankles covered. She realizes "for the first time, what, in other circumstances, she would have been taught as a child, that is to say, the sacred responsibilities of womanhood." We may theorize that Orlando was nurtured (as a boy?), was socialized into the values of some remote historical period (perhaps among medieval gypsies?), but in a fantasy such as this book is, we can see a

Utopian psychology in operation. Because Orlando arrives as an adult on the scene of each new era, she escapes normal childhood socialization; she escapes the limited vision of "home," of the one childhood world, domestically and socially, which usually gives human beings their primary values and loves. Orlando's ancestral home perhaps symbolizes these prerational attachments, but even this home, this symbolic place of comfort, changes size and decor with each era and becomes emblematic of Orlando's capacity for change even at a basic level, at the level of what "home" means, of what psychological comfort and security mean. With an adult's judgment, not a child's dependent need, Orlando views each era, and is thus free to let go of illusion after illusion with a minimum of anguish and a maximum of growth and self-renewal.

Orlando's change of sex, important as it is, is only one of many changes; her discovery of the limited role allotted to women is only one of several major disillusionments. The feminist issues, prominent in this novel and in some ways parallel to those discussed in *A Room of One's Own,* are placed in the quite positive context of an ongoing process of personal and social evolution, an evolution which this fantasy overturns stereotypical notions about sex roles as easily as stereotypical notions about the importance of personal fame or of social class. Because we have already seen her so readily and sensibly readjust to illusions about infatuation, fame and class, we are carried buoyantly onward by the momentum of suspended disbelief—and the momentum of the narrator's detachment and humor—when Orlando passes through the oppressive nineteenth century unscathed, having paid her dues to the "spirit of the age" by acquiring a wedding ring; she feels, however, as though she is crossing a border and carrying contraband, for she is a woman and yet she has smuggled a writer's mind into the nineteenth century.

—Judy Little, *Comedy and the Woman Writer: Woolf, Spark, and Feminism* (Lincoln, University of Nebraska Press, 1983): pp. 70–71.

PATRICIA CLEMENTS ON 'AS IN THE ROUGH STREAM OF A GLACIER': VIRGINIA WOOLF'S ART OF NARRATIVE FUSION

[Patricia Clements has taught Modern Literature at the University of Alberta. She has published on nineteenth- and twentieth-century poetry and prose, and co-edited a critical volume of Hardy's poetry. In this excerpt, Patricia Clements speaks on the role of the Great Frost in the novel.]

The Great Frost is central to the design of *Orlando* chiefly because it confirms in the character the figure of desire and betrayal. (It is not irrelevant to remember that Stendhal, in what John Middleton Murry called 'that curious book *De l'Amour*', names 'crystallization' that psychological process by which Venus becomes entirely attached to her prey.) The Frost is the basis for the book's important repetitions and rebirths. When the transformed Orlando returns to a transformed London, for instance, after leaving the gypsies, it is 'Sasha the lost, Sasha the memory' that she first encounters. When, Captain Bartolus at her side to name, among other monuments, Mr. Wren's new cathedral, she weeps to think, 'Here . . . had been the great carnival. Here, where the waves slapped briskly, had stood the Royal Pavilion. Here she had first met Sasha.' And she goes on to make the inevitable association: 'About here (she looked down into the sparkling waters) one had been used to see the frozen bumboat woman with her apples on her lap.' And when, much later, shopping by motorcar in Oxford Street, Orlando is deceived by a whiff of scent, she thinks:

> Time has passed over me . . . this is the oncome of middle age. How strange it is! Nothing is any longer one thing. I take up a handbag and I think of an old bumboat woman frozen in the ice. Someone lights a pink candle and I see a girl in Russian trousers.

The old bumboat woman, her lips hinting at subsurface truth, is carried along as the essential companion of the 'Sasha!' 'Faithless!' to whom Orlando calls through the centuries.

One of the truths the old bumboat woman hints at is death, of course, and, as the necessary partner of 'Sasha the memory', she hints at betrayal and loss in love: her blue lips suggest the real, the human changes underlying the fantasy. But I suggested earlier that the image of the frozen stream is an emblem of Woolf's own literary procedure, and the lips of the frozen bumboat woman hint at that, too. Her literary lineage, embedded with her in the ice, is both witty and thematically resonant. It leads by a plunge to the beginnings of the tradition in which the poet of 'The Oak Tree' writes, and by a return to Vita Sackville-West, whose feeling for Violet Trefusis supplies the material for the Sasha episode.

> —Patricia Clements, "'As in the rough stream of a glacier': Virginia Woolf's Art of Narrative Fusion," in *Virginia Woolf: New Critical Essays*, ed., Patricia Clements and Isobel Grundy (London, Vision Press, 1983): pp. 15–16.

⊗

## MADELINE MOORE ON *ORLANDO:* AN IMAGINATIVE ANSWER

[Madeline Moore has been a professor of English Literature at the University of California, Santa Cruz. She has published numerous articles on Jane Austen, Joseph Conrad and Virginia Woolf. In this excerpt, Moore speaks on fact and fantasy in the novel.]

Woolf's interest in biography was only a part of the larger aesthetic question which preoccupied her before and during the composition of *Orlando:* the question of how the dichotomy between fact and fancy affects not only biography, but also the novel and poetry, and how that dichotomy might be overcome.

In "The Narrow Bridge of Art' she predicts that in the future, the fact-recording power of fiction will decline. Fiction 'will resemble poetry [because] . . . it will give the relation of the mind to general ideas and its soliloquy in solitude'. Of the novelists she mentions, only Laurence Sterne in *Tristram Shandy* reveals this power. And in 'Phases of Fiction', the long article written simultaneously with *Orlando,* Woolf recognizes that Sterne, like the modern biographer, is as fascinated by the 'fancies and sensibilities' of his own mind as he is with Uncle Toby's character. 'In no other book are the writer and reader so involved together.'

Like Sterne, Woolf sought to explode the fact-bound nature of fiction by externalizing the self-consciousness of the author or 'biographer' herself. In Vita Sackville-West, she discovered a modern prototype whose complexity called for the self-conscious fantasies which permeate *Orlando*. But Vita's portrait is fantastic not only because the hero-heroine changes sex and defies time to gain autonomy; it is fantastic because Woolf externalizes the arbitrary nature of creation itself, as she satirizes her own powers of observation and the audacious notion that a life may be ultimately defined. Essentially, she wove an everlasting garland round her fickle lover in the reciprocal form of the novel itself. She eternalized her role as the pursuer, and Vita's role as the pursued through the machinations of the outwitted 'biographer' seeking constantly to unite the many selves of his elusive subject.

This double emphasis persists throughout *Orlando*. On the one hand the biographer is very much fascinated by his own sensibilities, and through his naïveté, Woolf gains a self-reflexive forum whereby she can ask the social and aesthetic questions which interested her most. On the other hand, her emphasis on the elusiveness and vigor of the human personality which, in the novel, persists through 428 years, allows her to connect her belief in pantheism with her faith that human talent will not be wasted, if given half a chance.

—Madeline Moore, *The Short Season Between Two Silences: The Mystical and the Political in the Novels of Virginia Woolf* (Boston, George Allen & Unwin, 1984): pp. 96–97.

# Plot Summary of
## *Between the Acts*

*Between the Acts,* Virginia Woolf's final novel, published after her death, opens on a summer evening as Mrs. Haines, the farmer Rupert Haines' wife, is speaking to Bartholomew Oliver, the eldest of his family, about the town cesspool. Bartholomew's daughter-in-law Isabel enters the room and says that she had been sitting with her son who wasn't feeling well. Isabel is intrigued by Rupert Haines and soon after she enters the room, indulges in a fantasy about him. Isabel's fascination is sensed by Mrs. Haines and a tension arises.

The narrative moves to the following morning with the introduction of Pointz Hall where the Oliver family has lived for over a hundred and twenty years. The narrative zeros in on Lucy Swithin, Bartholomew's widowed sister, who is talking to her brother, inquiring as to why the house was built in a hollow facing north. Lucy's mind is then swept into reflection about the environment and her family's history, and the reader is told that she is 'given to increasing the bounds of the moment by flights into past or future.'

As Lucy settles down to tea, the narrative follows the Oliver nurses as they walk in the woods with George, Bartholomew's grandson. George becomes captivated by the flowers and trees around him. His concentration is disrupted by his Grandfather who jumps out from behind a tree, pretending to be a monster from the woods. George gets frightened and begins to cry, leading Bartholomew to grumble about how his grandson is a cry-baby.

Isabel, George's mother, watches through her bedroom window as her son returns from the woods with his nurses. Isabel is brushing her hair and thinking about the feelings she had had the previous night for Rupert Haines, the farmer.

Bartholomew enters the house with his dog. Isa runs into him downstairs and her father-in-law tells her that George is a coward. Lucy, Bartholomew's sister, returns from church and reminds him that the pageant is today. They get into a conversation about the history of the pageant and what will take place given the various weather conditions. Isa laments about hearing the identical conversation every year, though she does not say anything aloud. Through their conversation, the reader is made aware that Lucy is very religious, while her brother is not.

As the Olivers are preparing for lunch, Mrs. Manresa, an acquaintance from the area, and her friend, William Dodge, come unannounced to their house. They are invited in and two more places are set at the table.

Giles Oliver, Isabel's husband, comes home and changes his clothes before joining the group. He had seen Mrs. Manresa's car in the driveway. The reader is told outright that Giles is the type of person whom Mrs. Manresa adores. Isabel is sensitive to Mrs. Manresa's adoration for Giles. Despite having felt something herself for Mr. Haines, she reflects on how she loves this man who is the father of her children.

Following lunch, the group decides to take their coffee out to the garden. Giles gets irritated about sharing the view with his aunt Lucy for whom he holds little respect. They talk about the pageant and how important the audience has been in past performances.

The narrative continues as Miss La Trobe, the writer, director and producer of the pageant, is pacing back and forth before the opening of the first act, contemplating the weather and looking over the materials for the play. The narrative jockeys between Miss La Trobe and the group at the Oliver's house. Through Woolf's attention to the internal musing of her characters, the reader is made aware of Giles' impatience, Mrs. Manresa's interest in him, Isabel's combination of love and hate for her husband, and Miss La Trobe's elated and distressed mood swings based on the fluctuating status of her art.

As the group at the Olivers' waits in the garden, Lucy decides to give William Dodge, Mrs. Manresa's guest, a tour of the house. Lucy seems to have sensed William's unease and treats him as graciously as she can. William is grateful for Lucy's kindness, feeling that she has helped him become more of a complete man.

When Lucy realizes that it's time to get to the pageant, they head off, arriving just after the prologue starts. They are told that the play is about English history and that there is a particular character meant to be England herself. The play gets underway and the audience is excited by the opening song that comes out of the gramophone. The performers start to act as if they are at a play, witnessing a different performance. Random scenes and lines persist throughout the opening and Isabel along with the others in her family have difficulty deciphering the events. Isabel decides that there are only two emotions, love and hate, and there is 'no need to puzzle out the plot.' She wonders if this is what Miss La Trobe was intending. There is more music and dancing and a seemingly random construction of scenes before the first break is announced.

The group gets up and strolls away from the pageant. Giles runs across a snake, choking with a toad in its mouth. He squashes it with his foot and feels a sense of relief at his action. He walks to the barn, blood splattered on his shoe. As more people gather in the barn for tea, Woolf shines her narrative light on the masks that people wear in public, speaking with fashionable expressions and expressing delight over the tea, 'disgusting though it was, like rust boiled in water, and the cake fly-blown. But they had a duty to society.'

William Dodge approaches Isabel and they engage in conversation until George, Isabel's son, approaches with his nurse. Isabel thinks about Giles and how their relationship is 'strained'. She wonders if he is as interested in Mrs. Manresa as she appears to be in him.

Woolf does a skillful job of highlighting the illusory nature of social interaction and perception as the narrative focuses on Mrs. Manresa who beckons Giles, imagining that the blood stains on his shoe are due to a valorous act he had performed for her. Isa and Giles, meanwhile, are engaged in a moment-to-moment struggle over the implications of their minuscule actions and words. Isa regards her husband's blood-stained shoes and stubborn attitude as childish. She decides to offer a tour of the greenhouse to William Dodge.

As they walk, Isa asks him if he's married. He immediately becomes self conscious, assuming she was able to guess, 'as women always guessed, everything.' Although nothing is stated explicitly, after the earlier references to his being half a man, and the scene in the greenhouse where Isa is seen as no more sexual than a statue, the reader and Isa are left to assume that William is a homosexual, coping in a repressed age.

The **second act** begins once everyone has returned to their seats. Soon after the play resumes, the wind picks up, making it difficult for the audience to hear. Miss La Trobe, who had been elated only minutes before, becomes instantly enraged, imploring her actors to sing and speak louder. But the wind grows even fiercer, drowning the actors' words out completely. Just when everything seems dead, the cows from the neighboring field start to bellow, as if on cue. 'The cows annihilated the gap; bridged the distance; filled the emptiness and continued the emotion.' Miss La Trobe reaches a state of elation once again until the bellowing stops and the audience looks at their programs instead of the stage.

Before the third scene is performed, the audience is informed that a scene had to be omitted. They are told what would have taken place and are asked to imagine it all. Following the next scene, there is another break. Giles asks Mrs. Manresa if she'd like a tour of the greenhouse. She accepts. Meanwhile, Lucy approaches Miss La Trobe and tries to express her pleasure in the performance, mentioning that she feels empowered by the play and a part of it. Isa takes a stroll on her own and picks a rose for herself. While walking beside the greenhouse, she sees her husband and Mrs. Manresa. She follows them back to the pageant where the next act is about to begin.

When the next scene ends, the ticking of a machine emanates from the stage. The audience discusses the meaning behind it all. The reader is told how unhappy Isa, Giles and William are, describing them as 'caught and caged; prisoners; watching a spectacle. Nothing happened. The tick of the machine was maddening.'

While the audience waits for the next act, there is discussion about how the proceeds go to help the church. They read about the next act which is labeled 'The Present Time. Ourselves.' Meanwhile, Miss La Trobe is observing her audience from behind the trees, fearing that her performance has been a failure—that she has not given the audience what they need. Then it starts to rain, suddenly, unexpectedly. But it stops just as suddenly, and music begins. But as with the rain, the music too ceases abruptly. And just as the crowd grows restless, actors jump out from the sides and run before the audience, holding pieces of a mirror, forcing the audience to gaze upon themselves. Most feel uncomfortable and divert their eyes, except for Mrs. Manresa who uses the opportunity to fix her hair and powder her nose.

When the irritability of the audience reaches its peak, and people start to gather their things to go, a voice rises from the bushes, projected through a megaphone. It starts to preach about how the multitudes of people that the mirrors are reflecting are all the same, filled with contradiction, hypocrisy and goodness, materialism and selflessness. Then the voice stops and music takes its place. It turns out to be the wrong record, so it's quickly changed and then just as quickly cut.

Overall, there are mixed emotions regarding the pageant's effectiveness and purpose. Rev. G. W. Streatfield stands up and though the crowd is apprehensive about what he might say, he expresses his mild confusion about the meaning. He offers his humble interpretation, suggesting that the play meant to imply that everyone is a part of the same thing, acting out different roles that are really the same, all existing within nature which plays a part of its own. He uses the angle of nature and higher influences to mention the church, asking the audience to consider making a contribution. 'Instantly collecting boxes were in operation. Hidden behind glasses they emerged.'

As the audience starts to leave, they discuss the various ways in which the play could be interpreted. The narrative focuses on Lucy and her brother Bartholomew as they walk back to Pointz Hall. Lucy asks if they should thank Miss La Trobe, but her brother brushes the idea off, claiming that they should thank the actors or themselves instead. They walk past a pond where Lucy gazes at the fish and feels a part of them, evoking the message that Rev. Streatfield suggested about the relationship between nature and man. Lucy thinks further about her faith, contrasting her beliefs with those of her brother who 'would carry the torch of reason till it went out in the darkness of the cave.' They are soon met by William Dodge who was searching for Lucy so he could thank her for her kindness. Isa watches as her husband waits with Mrs. Manresa for William to get into her car.

The narrative meets up with Miss La Trobe as she emerges from hiding. She starts cleaning up after the pageant and pauses beside a tree on the terrace where 'she had suffered triumph, humiliation, ecstasy, despair—for nothing.' Eventually she makes her way down to the local pub where she sits down in the smoke filled room with a drink and is struck by the first words of her next piece.

The narrative resumes in Pointz Hall where Lucy, Bartholomew, Isa and Giles are reflecting on the play, each having seen something different. Slowly the family returns to its normal routine, everyone resuming their customary roles. As the novel comes to a close, everyone goes off to sleep except for Isa and Giles who are 'left alone together for the first time that day.' The reader is told that even their roles are laid out neatly before them. 'Before they slept, they must fight; after they fought, they would embrace. From that embrace another life might be born.' The novel ends with a two-sentence paragraph:

'Then the curtain rose. They spoke.' ❀

# List of Characters in
## *Between the Acts*

**Bartholomew Oliver** is the eldest of the Olivers. In the beginning of the novel, he frightens his grandson George and is angered by the fact that George is not tougher.

**Giles Oliver** is Bartholomew's son. He is married to Isabel and is the father of George. He is a businessman who would prefer to work outdoors. He spends most of the pageant with Mrs. Manresa who is enamored by him.

**Isabel Oliver** is Giles' wife and the mother of George. In the beginning of the novel, she fantasizes about Rupert Haines. Though she wonders often about the relationship with her husband, she still feels genuine love for him and gets upset at how much time he spends with Mrs. Manresa.

**George Oliver** is the son of Isabel and Giles. He cries when his grandfather frightens him in the woods.

**Lucy Swithin** is Bartholomew's widowed sister. She is very religious. She is moved by the play and approaches Miss La Trobe at one point to tell her so.

**Rupert Haines** is a farmer about whom Isabel has a brief fantasy.

**Mrs. Haines** is Rupert's wife. In the beginning of the novel, she has a conversation about the town cesspool with Bartholomew.

**Mrs. Manresa** comes from out of town to see the pageant. She brings a guest, William Dodge, to the Oliver's house, but devotes all her energy toward Giles.

**William Dodge** is Mrs. Manresa's guest. He feels like half a man, but is consoled by the kindness of Lucy Swithin.

**Miss La Trobe** is the producer and director of the play. Her emotions, especially while the play is taking place, fluctuate from elation to profound distress.

**Mrs. Sands** is the Olivers' head servant.

**Reverend Streatfield** provides the pageant audience with a novice interpretation of the play, before asking for contributions for the church fund. ❀

# Critical Views on
## *Between the Acts*

[Joan Bennett has been an essayist, a scholar and a critic. She is the author of *Five Metaphysical Poets* and *Virginia Woolf: Her Art as a Novelist.* In this excerpt, Bennett speaks on the layered nature of the novel.]

In this book, after the partially unsuccessful expansiveness of *The Years,* Virginia Woolf returned to the severely disciplined form which is her special contribution to the art of the novel. It is a form which, because an apparently simple design is the vehicle of a complex experience, demands a close attention from the reader, such as is more usually accorded to poetry than to prose. As in poetry, certain effects depend upon the reader's response to sound sequences and to the multiple meanings and suggestions evoked by words and images. Other effects, however, depend, as in the traditional novel, upon character and situation.

The action is confined within twenty-four hours and takes place in one house and its surrounding estate. The central event is the historic pageant arranged to take place, on the terrace or in the barn according to the weather, as it has done annually for seven years. The main characters are the family who own the house, Mr Oliver, his son, his daughter-in-law, their two children and Mr Oliver's widowed sister Mrs Swithin, Miss La Trobe, the pageant mistress, and acquaintances who become part of the audience for the pageant. Minor characters include the servants of the house and the village community from the parson to the village idiot. This simple plot provides a viewpoint from which various aspects of the present are seen in relation to the past history of England. It allows also for the recurrence of certain themes which are important in the writer's vision of human life, such as the isolation of human beings, the rhythmic ebb and flow of love, the impulse to find or to create beauty order and significance.

The three main aspects of the subject are suggested by the title. At first it seems to refer only to the pageant, between the acts of which the human comedy is played. In the course of the book it becomes plain that it refers also to the interval, in which the action takes place, between the first and the second European war. The last words of the book make it clear that the title is also relevant to the emotional tension between Mr and Mrs Giles Oliver. Throughout the book there is an interval in their love. At the end they come together:

> "Left alone together for the first time that day, they were silent. Alone enmity was bared; also love. Before they slept, they must fight; after they had fought, they would embrace. From that embrace another life might be born. But first they must fight, as the dog fox fights with the vixen, in the heart of darkness, in the fields of night.
> "Isa let her sewing drop. The great hooded chairs had become enormous. And Giles too. And Isa too against the window. The window was all sky without colour. The house had lost its shelter. It was night before roads were made, or houses. It was the night that dwellers in caves had watched from some high place among rocks.
> "Then the curtain rose. They spoke."

> —Joan Bennett, *Virginia Woolf: Her Art as a Novelist* (Cambridge, Cambridge University Press, 1964): pp. 112–113.

ALICE VAN BUREN KELLEY ON *BETWEEN THE ACTS*

[Alice van Buren Kelley has been a professor of English at the University of Pennsylvania. She is the author of *The Novels of Virginia Woolf: Fact and Vision* and To the Light-house: *The Marriage of Life and Art.* In this excerpt, van Buren Kelley speaks on the roles and patterns in the novel.]

As Virginia Woolf's novels have progressed, the importance of pattern in life and in history has grown to represent the concrete manifestation of vision. So when Lucy demonstrates her awareness of this endless design, her role as "one-maker" is no longer in doubt. In her first appearance in *Between the Acts,* and in her last, she is shown reading her favorite book—an Outline of History—that tells of rhododendron forests in Piccadilly; when the entire continent, not then, she understood, divided by a channel, was all one; populated, she understood, by elephant-bodied, seal-necked, heaving, surging, slowly writhing, and, she supposed, barking monsters; the iguanodon, the mammoth, and the mastodon; from whom presumably, she thought . . . we descend.

Because she recognizes that men have not changed in essence from their first appearance on the earth, she understands the symbolic meaning of the pageant. "'The Victorians,' Mrs. Swithin mused. 'I don't believe,' she said with her odd little smile, 'that there ever were such people. Only you and me and William dressed differently.'" When someone asks, "'Was it an old play? Was it a new play?'" she answers somewhat enigmatically, pointing at the swallows, "'Look!'" "'They come every year,' she said, 'the same birds.'" "'They come every year,' said Mrs. Swithin, ignoring the fact that she spoke to the empty air. 'From Africa.' As they had come, she supposed, when the Barn was a swamp.'" Thus the swallows, the Outline of History, the pageant, and the people at Pointz Hall are all part of the pattern. By joining in the play, either as actors or audience, the characters in *Between the Acts* unconsciously reaffirm their unity with all other people and times. And Lucy understands. "'What a small part I've had to play!'" she exclaims to the authoress of the pageant. "'But you've made me feel I could have played . . . Cleopatra!'" If the others are puzzled or despairing at the fragmentation of humanity displayed in the act entitled "The Present Time. Ourselves" and need someone to interpret the scene for them, Lucy senses the pattern remaining firm below the surface.

If Bart and Lucy, in their roles as opposites living in the past, retain their affection for one another while maintaining their contrary ways of life, their nephew and niece do the same. Their relationship is a combination of love and hate, for the husband stands immovably for action and physicality while his wife represents contemplation and poetry. Because neither of them has faith in any established method of applying these theories to life, they both experience a greater sense of helplessness than do Bart and Lucy. Still these two, though having suffered a kitchen change from the reason and faith of their elders, continue to embody the opposing worlds of fact and vision.

—Alice van Buren Kelley, *The Novels of Virginia Woolf: Fact and Vision* (Chicago, The University of Chicago Press, 1971): pp. 231–232.

⟨𝒫⟩

## Allen McLaurin on Autonomy: 'Between the Acts'

[Allen McLaurin has been a teacher, critic and essayist. His works include *Virginia Woolf: The Echoes Enslaved*. In this excerpt, McLaurin discusses the influence of Roger Fry's writing on the novel.]

Fry's influence pervades *Between the Acts*. Bartholomew, like Fry, comments on the fact that the English are unresponsive to visual art. There is a discussion about two contrasting portraits, each representing a different kind of art. One is the portrait of an ancestor, and represents all the elements, which Fry was careful to distinguish from the truly aesthetic. It is a historical record and has only an antiquarian interest. Painted for a philistine, more interested in hunting than in art, it is not a genuine aesthetic object but what Fry would have called an 'opifact'. This Royal Academy anecdotal painting is contrasted with a genuine work, the formal excellence of which leads to silence:

> He was a talk producer, that ancestor. But the lady was a picture. In her yellow robe, leaning, with a pillar to support her, a silver arrow in her hand, and a feather in her hair, she led the eye up, down, from the curve to the straight, through glades of greenery and shades of silver, dun and rose into silence. The room was empty.

There follows a passage which, with its threefold repetition, mirrors the form of the novel as a whole. The image of the vase, a form which encloses nothing and which has no 'content', illustrates the central theme of Virginia Woolf's art—the emptiness at the heart of life which must be given shape and form: 'Empty, empty, empty; silent, silent, silent. The room was a shell, singing of what was before time was; a vase stood in the heart of the house, alabaster, smooth, cold, holding the still, distilled essence of emptiness, silence.' If we want dates and likenesses and names, Buster the horse and Colin the hound, then we must look, not to art, but to 'opifact', to the portrait of the ancestor.

Virginia Woolf's concern with self-consciousness at the time of writing *Between the Acts* was reinforced by her reading of Coleridge. In an essay written in 1940 she describes him as 'this Micawber' who 'knows that he is Micawber. He holds a looking-glass in his hand. He is a man of exaggerated self-consciousness, endowed with an astonishing power of self-analysis'. In order to get to the truth, she continues, we must 'have it broken into many splinters by many mirrors and so select'. In her pageant, Miss La Trobe tries to approach the truth in precisely this way. The disjointed language mirrors the meaning; it is a style, like that of Coleridge's letters 'pocketed with parentheses, expanded with dash after dash':

> Look! Out they come, from the bushes—the riff-raff. Children? Imps—elves—demons. Holding what? Tin cans? Bedroom candlesticks? Old jars? My dear, that's the cheval glass from the Rectory! And the mirror—that I lent her. My mother's. Cracked. What's the notion? Anything that's bright enough to reflect, presumably, ourselves?
> Ourselves! Ourselves!

In order to articulate reality it must be broken up in this way—it gains its value by being different from inarticulate intuition and sensation. Miss La Trobe's idea of holding up a broken mirror and other reflecting fragments is an attempt, perhaps, to capture the effect of Matisse's art as described by Fry:

> By the magic of an intensely coherent style our familiar every day world, the world where a model sat on a carpet, in front of Matisse's easel, has been broken to pieces as though reflected in a broken mirror and then put together again into a far more coherent unity in which all the visual values are mysteriously changed—in which plastic forms can be read as pattern and apparently flat patterns read as diversely inclined planes.

—Allen McLaurin, *Virginia Woolf: The Echoes Enslaved* (Cambridge, Cambridge University Press, 1973): pp. 54–55.

# SUSAN RUBINOW GORSKY ON PLOT AND PATTERN

[Susan Rubinow Gorsky has been a professor of English at Cleveland State University. Her articles and essays have appeared in such journals as *Modern Fiction Studies, Modern Drama,* and *The Journal of Popular Culture.* In this excerpt, Gorsky speaks on the immediate introduction of the novel's central topics.]

*Between the Acts* is Virginia Woolf's last novel, one of her best, and probably her bleakest. The entire action encompasses just about a day, but the chronological reference is nearly infinite. All the time man has known, however indirect that knowledge may be, is compressed into an allegorical pageant and the briefly glimpsed lives of a very few people. Three generations of the Oliver family reside at Pointz Hall, a country estate not far from London: Bartholomew Oliver, his widowed sister Lucy Swithin, his son Giles, Giles's wife Isa, and their son and daughter. About this nucleus revolve various others—a butler and cook, nursemaids, a delivery boy from the village, and Mrs. Manresa and William Dodge, unexpected luncheon guests. In the afternoon an event occurs of some importance to the village, the annual pageant which introduces numerous villagers and local gentry as actors and audience, with the author, Miss La Trobe, to direct the play and the Rev. G. W. Streatfield to summarize its meaning.

The first two scenes establish the novel's most important topics: the essential loneliness of the individual, and its apparent contradiction—the continuity of past and present, of man and his world. Rupert Haines (a "gentleman-farmer") and his wife talk with "Old" Mr. Oliver about a cesspool to be built in the neighborhood, at a site "on the Roman road." The novel occurs at such a time and place that it is possible to ride in an airplane in order to observe signs of the distant past: " the scars" left by the ancient Britons and Romans, by the Elizabethans, and by farmers during the Napoleonic wars. Even individual families have lived in the same location for generations, in some cases (like Mrs Haines) for centuries, with family graves in the church yard for proof. In contrast, the Olivers are relative newcomers, having lived in Pointz Hall "only something over a hundred and twenty years," with a portrait of "an ancestress of sorts" and a few family mementoes as proof of their place in history. Although Haines and his wife say little and do less, they unwittingly introduce

84

the second main theme. Isa, whose relation with her husband is a complicated mixture of love and hate, is attracted to Rupert Haines, usually referred to simply as "the man in grey." This reference underscores his personal insignificance to Isa; to her Haines is a fantasy symbol, much as Katharine Hilbery is at first to Ralph Denham. At some only partly conscious level, Mrs. Haines is aware of Isa's sexual response to Haines, so she is also tense. Isa is domestic, sophisticated, and civilized, but at the same time sensual, childish, and brutal; although frustrated she is willing to cause frustration in others. Like someone with a toothache she wants a "cure." At thirty-nine she is "the age of the century," and an apt symbol for the confusions of her age.

From this small group and intense opening, the novel contracts still further, so that the next morning begins with Lucy Swithin awakening alone in her room. Gradually the focus widens to take in first other members of the household and shortly later Mrs. Manresa and William Dodge. Mrs. Manresa is a middle-aged woman, "oversexed, overdressed," rather vulgar, but her exuberance is uncontrived; she is a "wild child," unashamed, as natural as the air. William is a nervous "gentleman" who seems an outsider, perhaps because he may be an artist or poet or perhaps because of his homosexuality. Isa feels drawn to the alien William, Giles and Mrs. Manresa feel a mutual physical attraction; within these parameters the afternoon wears on towards the pageant in alternating tension and quiet. But even the periods of quiet display numbness rather than peace.

> —Susan Rubinow Gorsky, *Virginia Woolf* (Boston, Twayne Publishers, 1978): pp. 128–129.

## SALLIE SEARS ON THEATER OF WAR: VIRGINIA WOOLF'S *BETWEEN THE ACTS*

[Sallie Sears has been a professor of English at the State University of New York, Stony Brook. She is has published books on Henry James and Sylvia Plath. In this excerpt, Sears explains how the most coherent communication in the novel is not delivered audibly.]

The few "authentic" (and coherent) communications that take place in the novel are in fact not audible. Most, furthermore, are hostile, as when Isa "overhears" Giles thinking about Dodge, the homosexual: "A toady; a lickspittle . . . a teaser and twitcher . . . not a man to have straightforward love for a woman—his head was close to Isa's head—but simply a—At this word, which he could not speak in public, he pursed his lips." In fact, however, he has not spoken *any* of these words aloud, including the "acceptable" ones. (The unacceptable one he cannot say even to himself. Nevertheless, Isa knows what the word is.) If, as in this instance, these silent utterances are "understood" by an equally silent auditor, the understanding and the communion remain tacit. Speech is frozen; dialogue is soundless. What R. D. Laing calls the "false self"—the self visible to the world (hence objectively "real") but dishonest in what it makes visible—is, though audible, incoherent; the "real self," though coherent, is mute. Encased in the language the characters use to keep reality at bay—a language that is false, inappropriate, theatrical—the gestures of that self leave little trace.

When painful subjects break past such inhibitions, speakers and listeners alike automatically turn off. Their attention flags; their thoughts wander; they interrupt themselves and one another. "Serious" talk quickly turns commonplace. When it doesn't, they help it to:

> And what about the Jews? The refugees . . . The Jews . . . People like ourselves, beginning life again . . . But it's always been the same. . . . My old mother, who's over eighty, can remember . . . Yes, she still reads without glasses. . . . How amazing! Well, don't they say, after eighty . . . (Elisions in original. Note that the conversation is back on "safe" ground immediately.)

Even those who want to speak openly to others cannot. Words fail them, or courage.

Moved by Lucy Swithin's kindness, Dodge longs to pour out his anguish:

> "At school they held me under a bucket of dirty water, Mrs. Swithin; when I looked up, the world was dirty, Mrs. Swithin; so I married; but my child's not my child, Mrs. Swithin. I'm a half-man, Mrs. Swithin; a flickering, mind-

divided little snake in the grass, Mrs. Swithin . . . but you've healed me. . . ." So he wished to say; but said nothing.

Like Mr. Ramsay seeking to embrace his dead wife, the characters grope in vain for living contact. All that is granted them is the momentary awareness of a lack, an absence, an incapacity, a lost vocabulary: "'We haven't the words—we haven't the words,' Mrs. Swithin protested. 'Behind the eyes; not on the lips; that's all.'"

"'Thoughts without words,' her brother mused. 'Can that be?'"; a passing sense of their own ineptitude ("I can't put two words together. I don't know how it is—such a chatterbox as I am with my tongue, once I hold a pen"; "Contemplating the idiot, Mr. Streatfield had lost the thread of his discourse. His command over words seemed gone").

—Sallie Sears, "Theater of War: Virginia Woolf's *Between the Acts,*" in *Virginia Woolf: A Feminist Slant,* ed., Jane Marcus (Lincoln, University of Nebraska Press, 1983): pp. 219–220.

## Evelyn Haller on Isis Unveiled: Virginia Woolf's Use of Egyptian Myth

[Evelyn Haller has taught English at Doane College in Crete, Nebraska. She has published critical works on Virginia Woolf and Willa Cather. In this excerpt, Haller speaks on the Egyptian themes in the novel.]

Of all her novels, *Between the Acts* has the most palpable Egyptian ambience. For example: "All was sun now. The view laid bare by the sun was flattened, silenced, stilled." Visually, the landscape of Pointz Hall has two dominant objects: the spire of Bolney Minster and Hogben's Folly. While the mode of emphasis of the former suggests the Quaker designation for church as "steeple house," both forms evoke the obelisk of Egyptian landscape reinforced by the punning name of the country house itself: "points hall." "Obelisk" was one of the words on Vita's list. Two obelisks were prominent in

Anglo-Egyptian relations. One, a red granite obelisk with a repeated inscription in hieroglyphics and Greek, had been discovered on the Island of Philae in1815 and brought to Kingston Lacy, a country estate in Dorsetshire. Together with the Rosetta stone, it gave Champollion evidence that hieroglyphics were more than a system of picture writing: they had over the centuries become increasingly phonetic. The other prominent obelisk, Cleopatra's Needle, had been brought to London through the generosity of Sir Erasmus Darwin, who was also to aid Amelia Edwards in founding the EEF. Woolf mentions Cleopatra's Needle in a draft of the 1910 portion of *The Years* as representing, among other things, the contrast of the long stretch of prehistory, with "our civilization . . . but the thickness of one green leaf on the top."

The pageant at Pointz Hall, which marshals through tableaux two millennia of English history (it can be surveyed in an afternoon), occupies the central space of the novel. The song the costumed villagers sing in winding procession, "Digging and delving . . . for the earth is always the same, summer and winter and spring; and spring and winter again; ploughing and sowing, eating and growing; time passes," corresponds to the rites of a significant June day in Greco-Roman Alexandria when a festival celebrated the day "when the star of Isis, Sothis, arose, this being regarded as New Year's Day. The rising marked three events simultaneously: the birth of a new year, the summer solstice, and the beginning of the inundation." The presence of this ancient festival can be discerned throughout the novel, but most specifically in the final panels as Miss La Trobe composes her next play. Between her initial vision of "two figures, half concealed by a rock" and their words unheard but alluded to in the final sentence, there is an allusion to the inundation of the Nile: "From the earth green waters seemed to rise over her. She took her voyage away from the shore." Lemprière states that "the Egyptians believed that the yearly and regular inundations of the Nile proceeded from the abundant tears which Isis shed for the loss of Osiris." Abundant tears had flowed during the pageant as metaphorically assigned rain down the cheeks of both Isa and Miss La Trobe. Isa, moreover, had searched for her husband Giles and repeatedly lamented the loss of her ideal lover Rupert Haines.

Miss La Trobe's "voyage away from the shore" suggests another festival: the Navigium Isidis (the Sailing of the Ship of Isis), "the extension of her power beyond Egypt." Pater, following Apuleius, describes how on one of the "first hot days" from many harbors "on the Mediterranean, the *Ship of Isis* went to sea, and every one walked down to the shore-side to witness the freighting of the vessel . . . its launching and final abandonment among the waves, as an object really devoted to the Great Goddess, the new rival, or 'double,' of ancient Venus." Classical sources also refer to "the procession on the banks of the Nile at Philae as the water begins to rise"; processions in honor of Isis feature mirrors similar to the spirit and fact of the mirror dance that closes the pageant at Pointz Hall. Apuleius has described the mirror bearers in Isiac procession; and the British Museum keeper contemporary with Woolf, Wallis Budge, informs us that, judging from the monuments, "it seems as if their movements consisted of a series of short, sharp jerkings of the legs and arms, and leaping into the air." Compare this interpretation with Woolf's description of the mirror carriers of the dance that concludes the pageant at Pointz Hall: "Out they leapt, jerked, skipped. Flashing, dazzling, jumping."

—Evelyn Haller, "Isis Unveiled: Virginia Woolf's Use of Egyptian Myth," in *Virginia Woolf: A Feminist Slant,* ed., Jane Marcus (Lincoln, University of Nebraska Press, 1983): pp. 115–117.

# Works by
# Virginia Woolf

*The Voyage Out.* 1915.

*Kew Gardens.* 1918.

*Night and Day.* 1919.

*Monday or Tuesday.* 1921.

*Jacob's Room.* 1922.

*The Common Reader: First Series.* 1925.

*Mrs. Dalloway.* 1925.

*To the Lighthouse.* 1927.

*Orlando: A Biography.* 1928.

*A Room of One's Own.* 1929.

*The Waves.* 1931.

*A Letter to a Young Poet.* 1932.

*The Common Reader: Second Series.* 1932.

*Flush: A Biography.* 1933.

*The Years.* 1937.

*Three Guineas.* 1938.

*Roger Fry: A Biography.* 1940.

*Between the Acts.* 1941.

*The Death of the Moth and Other Essays.* 1942.

*A Haunted House and Other Short Stories.* 1944.

*The Moment and Other Essays.* 1947.

*The Captain's Death Bed and Other Essays.* 1950.

*A Writer's Diary.* 1954.

*Virginia Woolf and Lytton Strachey: Letters.* 1956.

*Granite and Rainbow.* 1958.

*Contemporary Writers.* 1965.

*Collected Essays.* 1967.

*Mrs. Dalloway's Party.* 1973.

*The Letters of Virginia Woolf, Vol. One (1888–1912).* 1975.

*Freshwater: A Comedy.* 1976.

*Moments of Being.* 1976.

*The Letters of Virginia Woolf, Vol. Two (1912–1922).* 1976.

*The Diary of Virginia Woolf, Vol. One (1915–1919).* 1977.

*Books and Portraits.* 1977.

*The Pargiters: The Novel-Essay Portion of* The Years. 1977.

*The Letters of Virginia Woolf, Vol. Three (1923–1928).* 1977.

*The Letters of Virginia Woolf, Vol. Four (1929–1931).* 1978.

*The Diary of Virginia Woolf, Vol. Two (1920–1924).* 1978.

*The Letters of Virginia Woolf, Vol. Five (1932–1935).* 1979.

*Women and Writing.* 1979.

*The Diary of Virginia Woolf, Vol. Three (1925–1930).* 1980.

*The Letters of Virginia Woolf, Vol. Six (1936–1941).* 1980.

*The Diary of Virginia Woolf, Vol. Four (1931–1935).* 1982.

*The Diary of Virginia Woolf, Vol. Five (1936–1941).* 1984.

# Works About Virginia Woolf

Annan, Noel. *Leslie Stephen: The Godless Victorian.* New York: Random House, 1984.

Auerbach, Erich. *Mimesis: The Representation of Reality in Western Literature.* Garden City, New York: Doubleday Anchor Books, 1957.

Bazin, Nancy Topping. *Virginia Woolf and the Androgynous Vision.* New Brunswick, New Jersey: Rutgers University Press, 1973.

Beja, Morris, ed. *Virginia Woolf:* To the Lighthouse, *A Casebook.* London: MacMillan, 1970.

Bell, Quentin. *Virginia Woolf: A Biography.* New York: Harcourt Brace Jovanovich, 1972.

Bennett, Joan. *Virginia Woolf: Her Art as a Novelist.* Cambridge: Cambridge University Press, 1945.

Blackstone, Bernard. *Virginia Woolf: A Commentary.* London: Hogarth Press, 1949.

Chambers, R. L. *The Novels of Virginia Woolf.* London: Oliver and Boyd, 1947.

Church, Margaret. *Time and Reality: Studies in Contemporary Fiction.* Chapel Hill: University of North Carolina Press, 1963.

Clements, Patricia, and Grundy, Isobel, eds., *Virginia Woolf: New Critical Essays.* London and Totowa, New Jersey: Vision Press and Barnes and Noble, 1983.

Collins, Robert G. *Virginia Woolf's Black Arrows of Sensation:* The Waves. Ilfracombe, England: Arthur H. Stockwell, 1962.

Daiches, David. *Virginia Woolf.* New York: New Directions, 1963.

DiBattista, Maria. *Virginia Woolf's Major Novels: The Fables of Anon.* New Haven and London: Yale University Press, 1980.

Fleishman, Avrom. *Virginia Woolf: A Critical Reading.* Baltimore and London: Johns Hopkins University, 1975.

Freedman, Ralph. *The Lyrical Novel: Studies in Herman Hesse, André Gide, and Virginia Woolf.* Princeton: Princeton University Press, 1963.

Gadd, David. *The Loving Friends: A Portrait of Bloomsbury.* London: The Hogarth Press, 1974.

Ginsberg, Elaine K., and Gottleib, Laura Moss, eds. *Virginia Woolf: Centennial Essays.* Troy, New York: Whitson Publishing Co., 1983.

Guiguet, Jean. *Virginia Woolf and Her Works.* Translated by Jean Stewart. New York: Harcourt, Brace, 1966.

Hafley, James. *The Glass Roof: Virginia Woolf as a Novelist.* Berkeley: University of California Press, 1954.

Heilbrun, Carolyn G. *Toward a Recognition of Androgyny.* New York: Knopf, 1973.

Johnstone, J. K. *The Bloomsbury Group: A Study of E. M. Forster, Lytton Strachey, Virginia Woolf, and Their Circle.* New York: Noonday Press, 1954.

Kelly, Alice Van Buren. *The Novels of Virginia Woolf: Fact and Vision.* Chicago: University of Chicago Press, 1973.

Leaska, Mitchell A. *Virginia Woolf's Lighthouse: A Study in Critical Method.* New York: Columbia University Press, 1970.

Love, Jean O. *Virginia Woolf: Sources of Madness and Art.* Berkeley: University of California Press, 1977.

McLaurin, Allen. *Virginia Woolf: The Echoes Enslaved.* Cambridge: Cambridge University Press, 1973.

Majumdar, Robin, and McLaurin, Allen, eds. *Virginia Woolf: The Critical Heritage.* London and Boston: Routledge & Kegan Paul, 1975.

Marcus, Jane, ed. *Virginia Woolf: A Feminist Slant.* Lincoln and London: University of Nebraska Press, 1983.

Marder, Herbert. *Feminism and Art: A Study of Virginia Woolf.* Chicago: University of Chicago Press, 1968.

Matro, Thomas G. *Only Relations: Vision and Achievement in* To the Lighthouse. *PMLA* 99, no. 2 (March 1984): 212–24.

Meisel, Perry. *The Absent Father: Virginia Woolf and Walter Pater.* New Haven: Yale University Press, 1980.

Moore, Madeline. *The Short Season Between Two Silences: The Mystical and the Political in the Novels of Virginia Woolf.* Boston: Allen & Unwin, 1984.

Naremore, James. *The World Without a Self: Virginia Woolf and the Novel.* New Haven and London: Yale University Press, 1973.

Pippett, Aileen. *The Moth and the Star: A Biography of Virginia Woolf.* Boston: Little, Brown, 1955.

Richter, Harvena. *Virginia Woolf: The Inward Voyage.* Princeton: Princeton University Press, 1970.

Rose, Phyllis. *Women of Letters: A Life of Virginia Woolf.* New York: Oxford University Press, 1978.

Rosenthal, Michael. *Virginia Woolf.* New York: Columbia University Press, 1979.

Spilka, Mark. *Virginia Woolf's Quarrel with Grieving.* Lincoln and London: University of Nebraska Press, 1980.

Thakur, N. C. *The Symbolism of Virginia Woolf.* London: Oxford University Press, 1965.

Vogler, Thomas A., ed. *Twentieth Century Interpretations of* To the Lighthouse: *A Collection of Critical Essays.* Englewood Cliffs, New Jersey: Prentice Hall, 1970.

Woodring, Carl. *Virginia Woolf.* New York: Columbia University Press, 1966.

# Index of
# Themes and Ideas

65–66, 67–68, 69; plot summary of, 54–60; Sasha in, 53–54, 61, 69, 70; Marmaduke Bonthrop Shelmardine in, 58, 61

*TO THE LIGHTHOUSE,* 14, 34–53; William Bankes in, 35, 36, 37, 41, 47, 51–52; Lily Briscoe in, 35, 36, 37, 39–40, 41, 44, 47–48, 52; Augustus Carmichael in, 34, 37, 39, 41, 47, 48; characters in, 41–42; critical views on, 10, 11, 43–53; Minta Doyle in, 37, 38, 39, 42, 47; and life-affirming drive, 43–44; Mrs. McNab in, 39, 42, 43; memory in, 51–52; plot summary of, 34–40; and Post-Impressionist art, 52–53; Andrew Ramsay in, 37, 41, 47, 48; Cam Ramsay in, 37–38, 39, 41, 45, 47, 48; James Ramsay in, 34, 37, 38, 39, 41, 45–46, 47, 48; Mr. Ramsay in, 11, 34, 35–37, 38, 39, 41, 47, 48, 49–50, 52, 87; Mrs. Ramsay in, 34, 35, 36–37, 38, 39, 41, 43–44, 46, 47, 48, 49, 51, 52; Nancy, Rose, Jasper, and Roger Ramsay in, 37, 39, 42, 48; Prue Ramsay in, 38, 41, 48; Paul Rayley in, 37, 38, 39, 42, 47; and shared internal monologues, 45–46; and symbol and structure, 47–48; Charles Tansley in, 34, 35, 36, 37, 41, 47; Woolf's inspiration for, 49–50

WOOLF, VIRGINIA: biography of, 10, 13–14; and Pater, 10–12